History of New York City

A Captivating Guide to Historical Events and Facts You Should Know About NYC

Free Bonus from Captivating History (Available for a Limited time)

Hi History Lovers!

Now you have a chance to join our exclusive history list so you can get your first history ebook for free as well as discounts and a potential to get more history books for free! Simply visit the link below to join.

Captivatinghistory.com/ebook

Also, make sure to follow us on Facebook, Twitter and Youtube by searching for Captivating History.

Table of Contents

Introduction

With New York City's well-renowned reputation, it can be difficult to envision how the city of today came to be. Imagining the city without its storied skyscrapers is a challenge to visualize.

However, years ago, this piece of land that today is called New York City was one of nature. Over time, it became sparsely populated but still retained its natural vistas. With the arrival of the Europeans, much of the eastern coast of the United States was altered. New York City was no exception.

New York City mirrored much of the country's experiences through the American Revolution, Civil War, and world wars. New York City weathered the changes, emerging as a beacon of hope and change for many.

This introductory guide to one of the most famous cities in the world will take you on a journey. Explore how the earliest people came to live in the area, how New York City was a haven for revolutionaries during the lead-up to the American Revolution, and how 9/11 forever impacted the city.

Chapter 1 – The First New Yorkers

The history and legacy of New York City began tens of thousands of years ago. Shaped by the Ice Age and evolving landscapes that arose after the cold, true Native New Yorkers adapted to their changing environment. Research to obtain more detailed information about the prehistoric New Yorkers continues today. As archaeologists gather additional evidence from early historical eras, they increase their understanding of the early days of New York City.

Well before the Europeans "discovered" New York City, Indigenous people lived in the area. The climate and topography of the region gradually warmed as the Ice Age ended, making the lands more inhabitable for humans. The earliest cultures that lived in North America, particularly in the region of New York City, are classified as the Paleo-Indian, Archaic, and Woodland periods. Each time period is grouped by how people lived, the tools they used, and the foods they consumed. Artifacts that have been discovered by researchers provide the first chronology of New York City.

Humans first migrated to North America by crossing the Bering Strait as early as 12,000 BCE. Journeying from the western part of the continent, the nomadic hunters and gatherers followed the migratory patterns of the animals they hunted. During the Paleo-Indian era, early humans relied on mammoths, peccary, mastodons, and giant ground sloths. They also hunted and ate prehistoric horses and bison. Nuts, fruits, and other vegetation were a part of their diet as well.

Arriving in today's New York City, the Paleo-Indians found a topography vastly different from the vista of skyscrapers one can see today. The area was transforming from being covered with glacial ice into a forested landscape. In this terrain, the first New Yorkers found a land filled with the flora and fauna that they needed to exist. Due to their migratory nature, the small groups in which they traveled left few remnants of the time they lived in each location.

Paleo-Indians.
https://commons.wikimedia.org/wiki/File:Glyptodon_old_drawing.jpg

Archaeological evidence of mastodon remains found in the New York City area supports the idea that the Paleo-Indians did reside in this locale. Additionally, stone artifacts from that time period have been found in the region. Lithics from this prehistoric era are noted by the fluted points of their stone tools. These chipped projectiles were often tied to shafts fashioned from bones or pieces of wood. Atlatls, spear-like devices, were used to hunt large and small game. Relics from the Paleo-Indian era have also been discovered at sites in the New York City area.

New York City's next era is known as the Archaic period. From 7000 to 1000 BCE, Archaic cultures used hunting and gathering as a means of existence. However, the climate was warmer than the Paleo-Indian era, providing a larger array of plants and animals for the early New Yorkers to subsist on. Small groups continued to seasonally travel to different areas to best utilize the bounty of the land.

Migration patterns shifted during the Archaic period. The bands of hunter-gatherers began to traverse within a more defined area. Evidence shows that campsites were used repeatedly, which supports a seasonal pattern of hunting. Massive mammals previously hunted were decreasing in population as areas became more densely forested. Smaller game, such as deer, turkey, rabbits, and moose, provided sustenance for the early New Yorkers.

Another transition noted with the Archaic peoples is evidence of a shift to transient settlements. Temporary shelters were created. Remains of spring and summer fishing locations along waterways and fall and winter hunting camps in wooded areas have been discovered. As the scope of their travel area decreased, the population of the Archaic peoples increased.

With New York City's access to marine life, the Archaic people established many fishing camps throughout the area. Middens, which are piles of discarded shells, have been found in the Bronx and Manhattan and on Staten Island. The reliance on shellfish and marine life was another important adaptation of the Archaic people. This time period is also known for an increase in the sophistication of stone tools and weapons. Since the people moved seasonally, the beginnings of agriculture are credited to the Archaic cultures.

The period from 1000 BCE to 1500 CE is referred to as the Woodland period. During this era, there was a proliferation of farming. Crops grown by the Woodland peoples supplemented the fishing, hunting, and gathering that had long sustained the early New Yorkers. Beans, squash, corn, and pumpkins were grown throughout the areas in which Indigenous people lived.

Settlements were becoming less transitory with the expansion of agriculture. People established villages where they resided year-round. Situated near needed resources, seasonal or secondary campsites continued to be utilized for activities like fishing, hunting, or the formation of tools.

One benefit of more stable communities was the development of trade between different settlements. Resources that were not available in one region were traded for with another tribe. Ideas and techniques were also shared and exchanged. The Woodland period saw a shift from the use of atlatls and spears to bows and arrows. Tools evolved; they were crafted from a broader range of stone and animal bones. The use and formation of pottery evolved rapidly during this period.

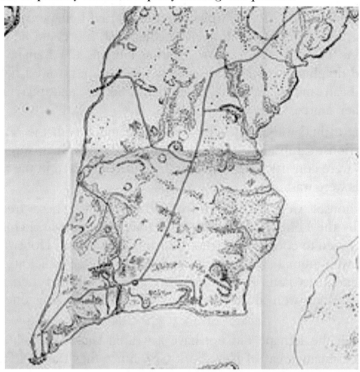

Native American paths in Manhattan.

During the Late Woodland period, many distinct Native American cultures were formed, one of which being the Lenni Lenape or Lenape. With a number of different translations, the name "Lenni Lenape" is usually translated to mean "original people" or "real person." However, the Lenape are often referred to as the Delaware. This is the name given to the Indigenous people by the English settlers. Sir Thomas West, the third Lord De La Warr, is credited with "finding" the river and bay, which are named after him, for the English.

The Lenape are considered to be one of the oldest tribes. Their land stretched from northern Delaware to eastern Pennsylvania, all of New Jersey, and southeastern New York. Lenapehoking, which means "place where the Lenape live," is their name for New York. Alternately, other researchers believe that the Lenape referred to the region as Scheyischbi, which means "place bordering the ocean." The island of New York City was called Manahatta or "hilly island."

Back then, Manhattan was a bounteous land of environmental riches. There were acres of forests, which the men of the Lenape used to hunt elk, bear, beaver, turkey, and deer. Shellfish and fish could be found in the waters near New York City. Marine animals the Lenape hunted included dolphins, whales, and seals. Lenape women sowed fields with squash, bean, and maize seeds. Wild plants, berries, and migrating birds were other sources of food in Manahatta.

Living a fluid way of life, the Lenape migrated with the seasons to their various campsites. Their buildings reflected their way of life. Shelters were constructed from natural resources located in the area. No materials were wasted.

Longhouses were fashioned from small trees. These trees were curved by the Lenape to create arches that framed their shelters. The bark was used to cover the longhouses from the weather. Doorways were covered with animal skins. Many families shared one longhouse, which was extended as families and clans grew in size. Other Lenape built wickiups, which were dome-shaped dwellings that housed one or two families.

Though the Lenape did not have a written language, their heritage remains in many areas of New York City. Since they traveled for trade, the Lenape created a vast system of pathways; some of these remain today as accessways throughout the city.

An extensive trade route of the Lenape started at today's Broadway. The Lenape walking trail to New York Bay was called Bredestraat by the Dutch for "wide street." Later, the English renamed the Lenape trail to Broadway. This accessway served as the starting route to trade with other tribes to the north of New York City.

Shatemuc, which means "the river that flows both ways," was the name given to the Hudson River by the Lenape. The water flows in a northerly and southerly direction in the estuary of the river. For the Lenape, Shatemuc provided access to trade with other Indigenous peoples. Cultures located along the river were within reach of the Lenape canoes.

Near the Hudson River, in today's Foley Square, the Lenape settlement of Werpoes existed. This location had access to a stream that flowed to the Shatemuc. Living here offered the Lenape land to grow their crops and a means to obtain fresh water.

Today's Pearl Street is so named because of the Lenapes' shell middens. These middens are great finds for us today, although the indigenous people of the past saw them as nothing more than mounds of trash. Archaeologists often find other artifacts, such as pottery pieces, tools, or sharpened stones used for weapons, in middens. Thus, even piles of trash provide tremendous insight into different cultures.

When the Lenape inhabited what became New York City, the harbor contained almost half of all the world's oysters. This area was a plentiful source of shellfish. After consuming the oyster from inside the shell, the used shells were discarded along the edge of the East River. Pearl Street was named by the Dutch settlers because of the bounty of pearls along the river. Discarded shells were eventually used to pave Pearl Street.

Throughout the city, there are a number of locations the Lenape used to gather with each other and trade. One important location was in today's Bowling Green. It was here that the Kapsee chief held council fires under the sacred elm tree, also known as the Council Elm. The Lenape gathered there to hear from their leaders and make decisions. Meetings were also a means to socialize and meet with other Lenape clans.

Other gathering sites used by the Lenape included today's Washington Square Park. Also used for farming, the Lenape called this area Sapohannikan, which means the "land of tobacco growth." As part of their seasonal migratory patterns, the Lenape traveled here in the spring for planting and in the fall for harvesting. The area was also a location for trading and social activities, such as music and playing games.

Kintecoying, or the "Crossroads of Three Nations," was located at Astor Place. Different factions of the Lenape traveled to attend meetings held here. Located on the eastern side of the Bowery were the village of Shempoes, between 10th and 14th Street near 2nd Avenue, and the village of Rehtanck, near Clinton and Montgomery Street. These settlements were home to the Canarsie tribe, which spoke Renneiu.

Another clan that joined the Canarsie was the Sapohannikan. Living on the west side of the Bowery, the village of Sapohannikan was situated on the Hudson River or Shatemuc. Located between Greenwich Avenue and Horatio Street, the Sapohannikan attended the Kintecoying.

The third language spoken by a different tribe of the Lenape at the Kintecoying was Munsee. They traveled from Shempoes village, which was north of Union Square. Once all the tribes arrived, meetings and sharing would have occurred near a sacred oak tree.

Oaks were revered by the Lenni Lenape. Legend tells of a tribal leader with a very ill wife. The tribe's shaman was not able to create a remedy to cure the ailing women. At the oak tree, the chieftain prayed to the Great Spirit to cure his wife. Upon his return to the village, the chief was met by his healthy and healed wife.

When the same chieftain's tribe was about to battle another tribe, he went to the oak tree to seek guidance from the Great Spirit. The directions the chieftain received were to offer gifts to the other tribe and ask for peace. Both were accepted.

Therefore, when the Lenape met, they gathered near a sacred oak. At the Kintecoying, the different tribes shared their traditional myths and stories with each other. Spiritual ceremonies were held. The latest news from each tribe was shared, and tribal councils were established to resolve any disputes between the tribes. Trade deals were conducted, and games, such as bagattaway (lacrosse), were played before the tribes returned to their separate settlements.

Not only were oaks sacred, but the Lenape also believed that everyone and everything had a soul. Trees, waterways, animals, flowers, and all life contained spirits. Therefore, treating all elements of the natural world with kindness was important. This helped frame their respect for the land and the natural resources they shared. Rituals were performed to pay homage to benevolent spirits. Other rites involved warding away unkind or evil spirits.

Settlements and housing were not built to be permanent structures. The Lenapes' reverence and respect for the land did not support the idea that the Lenape owned the land. Nature was to be shared and nurtured.

The Woodland period ended with the arrival of the first Europeans; then, the Contact period commenced. The world was forever altered for the Lenape.

The Contact period is considered to have taken place between the years 1500 and 1700. During these centuries, the Native Americans had large-scale and ongoing interactions with the newly arrived Europeans.

In 1524, the first encounter between the Lenape and a European is believed to have occurred. Lenape canoes met Giovanni da Verrazzano in New York Harbor. Sailing under the flag of France, Verrazano and his men were searching for the Northwest Passage. Due to weather conditions, Verrazano did not disembark from his ship and step on New York soil. Nevertheless, he claimed the land for France.

France did not pursue explorations in the area because of its battle with Holy Roman Emperor Charles V. So when Henry Hudson sailed into the harbor eighty-five years later, he was able to claim the land for the Dutch. Hudson, who sailed under the employ of the Dutch East India Company, was searching for a route to India. After he sailed up the river in his ship, the *Half Moon*, he realized that the waterway was not the way to China or India. To ensure that his trip was a success, Hudson landed in the Lenape home of Manahatta, which he claimed for the Dutch. Henry Hudson was the first European to set foot in today's Manhattan.

To make the trip even more rewarding for the Dutch East India Company, Hudson returned to Europe with beaver furs from the Lenape. Beaver fur was the current rage in Europe, so much so that by the end of the 1500s, beavers had been hunted to the edge of extinction. Hudson shared stories of the natural wealth of the lands that he discovered. This began a new trade route for the Lenape.

In 1621, the Dutch West India Company was founded by the Dutch Republic to encourage more trade and exploration. In 1624, twenty-five to thirty families were sent to New York to establish residency. They first built their homes on today's Governors Island, and the Dutch renamed the area New Amsterdam.

A few years later, the infamous land deal between the Lenape and Peter Minuit occurred. The Lenape did not believe they or anyone owned the land. Therefore, most researchers do not think the Lenape shared the same viewpoint on the transaction as the Dutch. The Dutch assumed that New Amsterdam was now their land, acquiring it for sixty guilders or twenty-four dollars in today's currency. It is now thought that the Lenape agreed to share the land and natural resources, which is why the deal was agreed upon under the Council Elm.

At the time of the Dutch settlers' arrival, it is estimated that the Lenape population was close to fifteen thousand. In less than one hundred years, the Lenape population in Manahatta would rapidly decline to only around two hundred. In addition to the depletion of natural resources, European diseases like smallpox and measles decimated many of the Indigenous people. Other Native New Yorkers were forced to relocate to survive the European onslaught.

Chapter 2 – They Came and They Stayed: The Expansion of the Europeans

Henry Hudson's explorations were financed and supported by the Verenigde Oostindische Compagnie or VOC. This international corporation helped unify the Dutch and its enterprises against other strong European powers. During this period in history, known as the Dutch Golden Age (c. 1575–1675), the Dutch were one of the wealthiest countries in the world.

Also known as the Dutch East India Company, the VOC's sponsorship of Hudson and his crew, who sailed on *Halve Maen,* or *Half Moon,* enabled Dutch expansion into the New World. Since Hudson, who was an Englishman, sailed under the flag of the Netherlands, the bounty of natural riches that he discovered was assumed to be under the control of the Dutch.

Replica of Halve Maen.
https://commons.wikimedia.org/wiki/File:Halve_Maen_front.jpg

Once merchants in the Netherlands received details of the seemingly endless resources available, entrepreneurs established the New Netherland Company. Quickly, towns, trading posts, and forts were constructed along the Hudson River by the newly formed company.

The New Netherland Company had a monopoly on the fur trade until 1618. During these four years, the main activity and goal of the Dutch was to maximize the trade potential of their charter. After the charter expired, the Dutch government did not renew it. It was busy negotiating with another group of traders that wanted to establish the Dutch West India Company.

Seeking to control the trade in the area and colonize the land, the Dutch leaders granted a twenty-four-year monopoly to the Dutch West India Company. In addition to gaining trading domination, the company acquired land that they called New Netherland.

One of the first areas the Dutch West India Company began settling was on today's Governors Island. At this point in history, the island covered seventy acres. The Lenape, who were the seasonal inhabitants of the island, called it Paggank or Nut Island. In the early 1600s, Paggank was named for the variety of nut trees that forested the land. The island was covered with hickory, chestnut, and oak trees. The Lenape used the land seasonally for their fishing camps.

When the Dutch arrived, they called the island Noten Eylandt, using the Lenape name. To facilitate the fur trade, the Dutch constructed a fort and a sawmill on the island in 1624. Many of the settlers moved to the larger Manhattan Island after a year. The fort and sawmill continued to operate while the Dutch controlled the area.

The move to Manhattan allowed for more farming, land for livestock, and fresh water. Fort Amsterdam was established in 1625. Six more ships sailed for New Netherland in 1625. In June of the same year, Governors Island received forty-five more settlers from three of those ships. Supplies, livestock, and horses also began to populate Noten Eylandt.

Following the move of many of the settlers from Paggank to New Amsterdam, the Dutch West India Company named Peter Minuit as director general of the colony. Minuit attempted to authorize the Dutch occupation of Lenape land with the infamous purchase of Manhattan. Since the Lenape did not believe people owned the land, they viewed the sale as an agreement to share. Eventually, this misunderstanding would lead to conflicts between the settlers and the Native Americans.

From the Dutch perspective, the growth of the settlement proceeded slowly. The Dutch West India Company sought to encourage more colonists to move there and reduce their costs. One solution that the Dutch West India Company developed was the Patroonship Plan in 1628. Under this plan, a patroon was granted land that they could settle. Patroons were landowners who were granted the same rights as owners of manors in Europe.

Patroons were expected to bring others to New Amsterdam and absorb the costs. There were restrictions on the new inhabitants. They could not join the fur trade or fish in the area. These remained under the tight control of the Dutch West India Company.

As adjustments were made to the Patroonship Plan, additional settlers joined the Walloons, who were the first thirty families. Most of the

Walloons agreed to work with the Dutch West India Company to settle New Amsterdam to escape religious persecution.

The lands that the Dutch West India Company's settlers were living on continued to expand. As they expanded, their farms and forts continued to encroach on lands that the Native Americans called home. Under the leadership of Director Willem Kieft, growing tensions between the Native Americans and the new arrivals erupted.

Willem Kieft.

Dutch government officials became increasingly interested in developing the settlement of New Amsterdam, located in the colony of New Netherland. Therefore, the government began to pressure the Dutch West India Company to relinquish some of its monopolistic control over the land and trading. As the company acquiesced to the government's demands, more settlers continued to arrive.

After the Dutch States General increased opportunities for settlers in the territory, the population increased. Not only did immigrants arrive from Europe, but settlers from other areas in the New World also went to New Amsterdam and New Netherland for entrepreneurial prospects.

Appointed as director in 1638 by the Dutch West India Company, Willem Kieft was selected for his business acumen. Kieft had no governing experience, so he entered a realm that he was not fully prepared for. His leadership style quickly created antagonistic relationships.

Those who had been living in New Amsterdam and New Netherland were accustomed to participating in the local government. With the mounting pressure of a dramatically increasing population, insufficient land, and an autocratic leadership style, Kieft's early tenure as director was tumultuous.

Adding to Kieft's expanding problems was his need for funds. Seeking to raise funds to fortify the settlement and increase the revenue generated by the colony, Kieft levied new taxes. Part of his tax plan included tributes from the Native Americans. These payments were allegedly to provide protection for the Native tribes from other Native Americans in the region. Leaders of the local tribes refused to pay Kieft's government. The Lenape and others believed they were sovereign nations that did not need protection from the Dutch.

Angry with the rebuke from the Native Americans, Kieft strung together a series of minor skirmishes with the Indigenous peoples as a justification to attack. In 1643, Dutch West India Company soldiers slaughtered members of the Lenape as they slept. One site of the massacre happened at Corlears Hook, which is part of the Lower East Side of Manhattan. It is believed over one hundred Native Americans were killed. This incident ignited Kieft's War.

For two years, ongoing battles and skirmishes between the Dutch and the Lenape occurred. Though the settlers participated in the initial attacks, many soon withdrew their support of Kieft's actions. He was held accountable for the damage and destruction caused by the continual raids. Finally, the Treaty of August 30 ended the conflict. During the war, it is estimated that more than 1,500 Native Americans died. Fewer than one hundred settlers perished.

For the Indigenous people of New Netherland, this episode began the eventual loss of their homeland.

Local leaders among the Dutch population successfully sought the removal of Kieft from the role of director (a role that was similar to governor). He was replaced in 1647 by Peter Stuyvesant, who served in that role until 1664. Stuyvesant found that New Amsterdam (and New Netherland) needed restoration.

Swiftly, he established himself as a strong leader who did not seek input from others. Stuyvesant transformed New Amsterdam into a Dutch enclave. A mixed population lived in New Amsterdam. All classes of Dutch society were represented there: immigrants from many countries in Europe, bonded and indentured servants, and enslaved Africans. At least eighteen languages were spoken among its residents.

Stuyvesant's aristocratic background and strict approach to governing caused him issues with the more democratic population. The Dutch government and the Dutch West India Company selected Stuyvesant to ensure that New Amsterdam generated profits. The combination of his leadership style and desire to please the company separated Stuyvesant from his constituents.

Stuyvesant modeled the government after the one found in Holland. In an attempt to placate the citizenry, Stuyvesant appointed an advisory council, the Nine Men. However, he and the council usually disagreed. Throughout his tenure, Stuyvesant governed as he believed was right, with the goal of creating a profitable community.

During the eighteen years that Stuyvesant led New Amsterdam, the population of Europeans and their descendants grew dramatically from two thousand to eight thousand. He worked to clean up the emerging city by rebuilding the streets and deterring citizens from dumping their trash in the streets. Additionally, Stuyvesant stopped pigs from digging at the base of buildings.

Structures in New Amsterdam were built from wood, so he sought to have them fireproofed. He supported churches, which began to establish schools to help control the ruffian youths. To support commerce, Stuyvesant formed a system to value wampum, Native American currency, and created a standardized measurement for bread so it could be controlled and sold by size and weight. A weekly farmers' market was also started under the directive of Stuyvesant.

Part of Stuyvesant's approach to instilling law and order in New Netherland was restricting religious freedom. This led to confrontations between Stuyvesant and leaders of various religious groups. Disagreements became so severe that Dutch West India Company leaders instructed Stuyvesant to relinquish his attempts to control the churches. He was to focus solely on trade and profits.

Clashes between Stuyvesant and town leaders also developed and increased in intensity. The advisory council attempted to send citizen complaints and concerns about Stuyvesant's oppressive reign to the States General in Holland. They were thwarted by Stuyvesant. However, the group, led by Adriaen van der Donck, persisted and met secretly. So, Stuyvesant had van der Donck arrested. After his release, van der Donck and other members of the advisory council went to Holland to present their complaints.

Though the advisory group was not initially successful, its members continued to rally to gain more input in the governing of New Netherland. Eventually, the Dutch West India Company and the States General conceded because they were afraid of losing complete control over New Netherland.

Stuyvesant was directed to form a municipal government for New Amsterdam. In 1653, New Amsterdam was incorporated as a city, which included a schout, two burgomasters, and five shepens. This structure of government is similar to installing a sheriff, two mayors, and five city councilmen. Together, they shaped the legislative and judicial governing bodies of New Amsterdam.

Another legacy from Stuyvesant's tenure was constructed in 1653. Fearful of attacks from the English, the pirates, Native Americans, and colonists from other European colonies that surrounded New Amsterdam, a protective wall was built. Nine feet high and 2,340 feet long, this fortification was built with 15-foot-long timber planks. The structure stretched from Pearl Street to Wall Street. Cannons were added for protection. Taxes from citizens paid for de Waal Straat.

Painting of New Amsterdam's Wall Street.
https://commons.wikimedia.org/wiki/File:Wall_Street_IRT_008c.JPG

New Amsterdam's first Jewish residents arrived the following year. They had been living in Brazil after being ousted from Spain and Portugal during the reign of Ferdinand and Isabella. They had moved to Holland, where they could practice their religion. When Holland captured Brazil as a territory, part of Holland's Jewish population relocated.

In 1654, Portugal seized control of the Dutch territory of Brazil, and the Portuguese ousted the Jewish population from the territory. Sixteen ships full of Jewish refugees sailed from Brazil. One ship, the *St. Catherine,* was captured by Spanish pirates. Rescued by a French privateer, those aboard the ship were charged with the cost of the passage. Lacking the funds to sail to Holland, the exiles were brought to the nearest port, which was New Amsterdam.

Stuyvesant wanted to refuse the ship and its inhabitants. However, the Dutch West India Company denied his request. The governing board of the company had many Jewish investors. Reluctantly, Stuyvesant complied, but he did restrict their freedoms and ability to trade with others. This continued to alienate Stuyvesant from his more open-minded citizens.

Despite the rift, New Amsterdam was a profitable location. By 1664, almost nine thousand people resided in the colony; it is estimated that only half of the population was actually Dutch. Holland's successes caused a growing rivalry with other European countries that were establishing their own vast network of colonies in North America. England and Holland sparred as the profits of the Dutch increased. England coveted New Amsterdam and New Netherland for their prime location. The Dutch colony was situated between other holdings of the English.

In 1664, the English arrived on the shores of New Amsterdam. Leading the English naval fleet was Richard Nicolls, who demanded Stuyvesant relinquish control of New Amsterdam. Initially, Stuyvesant refused. However, the ongoing rift between Stuyvesant and his constituents contributed to the demise of New Amsterdam. Stuyvesant was not able to assemble enough troops or citizens willing to support him.

Painting of the fall of New Amsterdam.

Without firing one shot, the English acquired New Amsterdam. Terms of the acquisition were negotiated between Nicolls, Stuyvesant, and the leaders of the community. In the "Articles, Whereupon the Citty and Fort Amsterdam and the Province of the New Netherlands Were Surrendered," citizens could remain on their land. Religious freedom and toleration would continue under the new regime. The newly installed governor Nicolls crafted the Duke of York's Laws in 1665 to create a more uniform code in the colony and the city of New York.

Another component of the agreement permitted all those currently in the roles of magistrates to remain in their positions. In court and council, transactions and communications were completed in a blend of Dutch and English. The next election would see more significant changes occur.

One key transformation made by the English was the renaming of New Amsterdam. Instead, it was named New York after King Charles II of England's brother, the duke of York.

The following year, New York began to evolve into a more English colony. The duke of York put forth a declaration that detailed the formation of a new governing body. On June 12th, 1665, the Dutch government's control of New York formally ceased. The first mayor of New York, Thomas Willet, was installed into office.

Conflict between the Dutch and the English continued. Battles were mainly fought at sea and ebbed and flowed for years. In 1672, the Third Anglo-Dutch War commenced. Europe and the East Indies were key battle areas in this war.

However, a Dutch fleet led by Jacob Benckes and Cornelis Evertsen sought to take back New York from the English. Their convoy of eight ships sailed into New York Harbor, catching the English by surprise. Soon, New York was once again under Dutch rule. It was renamed New Orange for Prince William of Orange. The government was changed back to the Dutch system. Members of the governing council were replaced by the Dutch.

For eighteen months, New Orange thrived. However, the Treaty of Westminster, which was negotiated to end the Third Anglo-Dutch War, included transferring New Orange back to the English. In early 1674, New York City reemerged and has retained its name since then.

Chapter 3 – The Seeds of Change

With the British regaining control of New York in 1674, laws governing the city came forth from King Charles II. His directive was to reinstate the Duke's Laws as the legal system in New York. This was met with resistance by the colonists, who sought a more representative form of government.

It was not until James, Duke of York, appointed Thomas Dongan governor in 1682 that the people of the colony of New York and New York City began to have their voices heard. Dongan replaced Edmund Andros, who left office with disenfranchised citizens and a colony that was struggling financially.

The duke of York empowered Dongan to convene a legislative assembly. All laws and agreements that were created by the assembly, passed by the representatives, and approved by Dongan were binding legislation stipulated by the duke. If the duke of York opposed any of the laws that were passed, he had the right to overturn them. Until that point, the agreed-upon legislation was legally binding in the colony and the city of New York.

In October 1683, eighteen men were elected to attend the first representative assembly in New York. For three weeks, the assemblymen met at Fort James in Manhattan. At the end of their session, the delegation of representatives agreed to and passed the Charter of Liberties and Privileges with the urging and support of Dongan.

Dongan approved the charter, which is often referred to as Dongan's Charter. The charter's provisions were immediately enacted.

Furthermore, the assembly's and Dongan's stipulations in the charter included the governmental structure, which called for a governor, a council, and an assembly of representatives. Dongan's Charter framed other rights involving religious toleration, the right to vote, and a trial by jury. Additionally, citizens could not be taxed without representation, and residents were not required to house soldiers without their consent.

Specifically for New York City, the charter created it as a self-governing entity. New York City was divided into five inner wards and one outer district. Each ward was authorized to vote for its own alderman, his assistant, assessors, and a constable. The inner wards were sectioned into North, East, South, West, and the Dock. The remaining sections of the city were consolidated into the outer ward.

As a note, the population permitted to vote was limited to White landowning men.

In 1685, King James II, the former Duke of York, succeeded Charles II. The following year, James formed the Dominion of New England and consolidated his control of Rhode Island, Connecticut, New Hampshire, and Massachusetts. James added New York and New Jersey to the Dominion of New England in 1688. Prior to this step, James dismissed the representative Assembly of New York.

Thomas Dongan was released from his role when New York was annexed into the Dominion. New York's colonial seal was broken in a symbolic gesture that illustrated the dramatic change in the type of government.

Edmund Andros assumed control of New York in 1688. He eliminated the representative government, decreed the Church of England as the Dominion's authorized religion, and raised taxes.

In England, the Glorious Revolution caused the absolute monarch, James II, to relinquish the throne. Once news of William of Orange and Mary assuming the monarchy reached the colonies, Governor Andros and other leaders of the Dominion were arrested and sent to England.

After the leaders selected by James II were overthrown, there was a power vacuum. In New York, support was divided between those who favored James II and William.

Rumors circulated that the followers of James II were planning to capture Fort James. Others speculated that current leaders were planning to burn the city. Another group of residents believed they had heard that James II's followers were plotting to massacre everyone who was of

Dutch lineage.

Residents sought the leadership of Jacob Leisler. Leisler was a commissioner, a justice of the peace, and a militia captain during Dongan's tenure. The Leislerians, the group led by Jacob Leisler, took control of Fort James and renamed it Fort William for the new king of England.

The rebels stated that their intention was to control Fort William until new leaders selected by William arrived from England. In the meantime, Leisler and his followers formed the Committee of Safety. This committee was established to govern New York. Jacob Leisler was chosen as the leader of the provisional government, and he appointed himself as acting lieutenant governor.

As an interim government, Leisler and his supporters worked to restore the rights they had before James II's oppressive reign.

Additionally, Leisler acted upon the fears that he and his constituents had about Roman Catholics. The group believed that Catholics were gathering forces to act against England and its laws. Leisler and his rebels justified their actions, and a millenarian movement that fostered the belief that the Second Coming of Christ grew in strength. The expanding suspicion of Catholics was further exacerbated by the conflict between the Catholic forces of Louis XIV of France and William of England. Concerns about the French actions in New York led Leisler to have all Catholics imprisoned.

King William selected Henry Sloughter as the new governor of New York. Sloughter's departure from England was delayed, so there was a significant time lag between the announcement and his arrival. Lieutenant Governor Richard Ingoldesby arrived in Manhattan before Sloughter. In January 1691, Ingoldesby ordered Leisler to vacate Fort James, which the rebels called Fort Williams. They refused because Ingoldesby was not the governor. The city was on the verge of a civil war, and tensions continued to escalate.

Ingoldesby and his troops returned to Manhattan in March and attacked the fort on the 17th. Two of Ingoldesby's soldiers were killed. Several were wounded.

A tense standoff between the forces lasted until Governor Henry Sloughter arrived in New York a few days later. After establishing his leadership council, Sloughter demanded that Leisler and the other rebels surrender. Leisler refused to surrender the fort. Some sources say that

Leisler declined because it was dark, so he waited until the next morning. Others say that Leisler needed to be convinced that Sloughter was truly who he claimed to be.

With either turn of events, when Leisler and his group turned themselves into the new governor, they were promptly arrested. Charges of treason were levied against Leisler; his son-in-law, Jacob Milborne; and eight others. The crime was due to the rebels retaining control of the fort and using force against government officials, which resulted in the death of two soldiers.

The trial was held in New York City in April 1691. Leading the case for the prosecutors were foes of Leisler and the other defendants. Leisler and his co-defendants proclaimed their innocence throughout the trial. They believed they had acted in good faith and secured Fort James and the government in the name of the English Crown.

Guilty verdicts were bestowed upon Leisler, Milborne, and six of the other eight defendants. Two of the rebels were acquitted of all charges. Eventually, all of the rebels were pardoned for their actions except their leaders.

Leisler and Milborne were sentenced to be hanged, disemboweled, decapitated, and quartered. Before the largest crowd in New York City up to this date, both men were hanged on May 16th, 1691.

Leisler's followers believed that the trial had not been conducted fairly and that the sentences were unjust. In 1695, both Leisler and Milborne were cleared of all charges. Their estates, which had been confiscated, were returned to their heirs. The bodies of the two leaders of Leisler's Rebellion were honorably reinterred at Manhattan's Dutch Reform Church on Garden Street.

Leisler and his execution served to demonstrate the depth of the divide in New York City. Leisler's Rebellion proved the city's and area's support of William. It also supported the creation of a regional council. Leisler's impact on Catholics would be felt for years, and the ban on Catholicism remained in effect until 1783.

Their deaths did not end the conflict between Leisler supporters and foes, the Leislerians and anti-Leislerians, respectively. For decades, the two groups continued to be bitter rivals over the government's structure.

Another colonist charged with sedition who would have an impact on the history of New York City was William Bradford. Bradford was a printer in Philadelphia, and he published a broadside that was deemed treasonous by Pennsylvania's Governor Blackwell. Broadsides were single sheets of paper; they had public announcements or advertisements on them. In 1692, Bradford was tried and jailed for his act of sedition.

After his release from prison, Bradford was lured to New York City with the promise of greater freedom of the printing press than he had in Philadelphia. His position as royal printer for the colony began in 1693 when he began operating the first printing press in New York City on Pearl Street. Bradford published New York's first newspaper, the *New-York Gazette*, in 1725.

Bradford continued creating controversy in his role as a printer. His first broadside that protested slavery was the "Catalogue of Fees." Later, Bradford printed the *Book of Common Prayer* in the Mohawk language. The prayer book was used by missionaries. New York's first set of published laws is also attributed to Bradford, who added page numbers to each of the pamphlets. His innovation enabled legislators to have the consecutive pages of laws bound together.

One of Bradford's more well-known legacies was his former indentured servant, John Zenger. In 1733, Zenger opened his own newspaper in New York City, *The New York Weekly Journal*, which competed against Bradford's paper.

Articles in Zenger's paper frequently and fiercely criticized William Cosby, New York's governor. Foes of the governor viewed him as a corrupt British official. Cosby attempted to increase his salary by taking part of the previous governor's pay. When the colony's supreme court ruled against Cosby, he replaced the chief justice. Zenger's paper was relentless in its attacks on Cosby and his actions.

Criticisms of British officials during the colonial era were illegal and considered treasonous. In November 1734, Governor Cosby demanded that Zenger be arrested and jailed for libel.

James Alexander and William Smith were Zenger's first attorneys. However, they were both found in contempt and disbarred by the court before the trial even began. The trial was expected to be so contentious that no other New York lawyer would choose to represent Zenger. John Chambers, an inexperienced lawyer who supported Cosby's administration, was selected by the court to defend Zenger.

Though Alexander and Smith were disbarred, they continued to fight for Zenger. The duo was able to retain the well-respected attorney Andrew Hamilton from Philadelphia to defend Zenger. As a note,

Andrew was not related to Alexander Hamilton. On August 4th, 1735, Zenger's trial began in New York City Hall. His defense was built on the assertion that derogatory statements are not libelous if the statements can be proven as true.

During the trial, Hamilton made a case for his client by talking directly to the jury. In his arguments, Hamilton reasoned that truthfulness and veracity are protections against defaming statements. Zenger published statements about the governor that people could verify. Hamilton was confident that the jurors would have the ability to determine the difference between truths and falsehoods. Harmful or derogatory truths were still honest statements; therefore, they were not seditious libel.

With only ten minutes needed to deliberate, the jurors found Zenger not guilty, and he was acquitted of all charges. One of the foundations of the Bill of Rights, freedom of the press, stemmed from this jury's decision. It would not be until the American Revolution that colonists would be able to embrace this freedom.

In the immediate aftermath of the trial, the British government tightened its grip on the budding rebellion. However, more seeds of revolutionary fervor were still sown.

Not only did newly arrived immigrants seek to create change in colonial New York City, enslaved people also sought to better their lives. Two uprisings of enslaved people occurred prior to the American Revolution, with the first revolt happening in the city on April 6th, 1712.

Of the approximately seven thousand inhabitants of New York City in 1712, one thousand were enslaved. In the densely populated area, enslaved people often interacted with other enslaved people. They also lived and worked near free people and indentured servants. Therefore, communications between groups were more easily facilitated, as was viewing the vast disparity between inhabitants of the city.

Rising hostility between enslaved people and their owners ignited on the night of April 6th, 1712. Twenty-three Black men gathered and set fire to a slaveowner's outhouse on Maiden Lane. The slave owner was Peter van Tilburg. Flames from the fire were a signal to other enslaved people to join the revolt.

As the fire spread, White people living in the area attempted to quell the blaze. When the White people rushed from their homes, rioters attacked them with guns, knives, and axes. Shots were fired into the growing crowd of White people. By the end of the revolt, at least eight White people were dead, and more than a dozen were wounded.

Governor Robert Hunter of New York sent the militia to end the melee. Rioters tried to escape, but they were hunted down. At least twenty-seven rebels were captured after they were found near Canal Street. Knowing that they faced horrific trials and captivity, six of the insurgents committed suicide. Forty of the insurrectionists were brought to trial. A few were acquitted and pardoned.

The other rioters suffered brutal executions. Most of the executions involved publicly performed torture beforehand. In total, twenty-one enslaved people were slain for their role in the rebellion. Their heads were displayed on stakes in the middle of New York City for all to witness.

Even stricter slave codes were promulgated in response to the uprising. Enslaved people were no longer permitted to marry or socialize. Taxes were increased on slave owners who wanted to free their enslaved people, which made doing so too costly. Freed Black people had their land taken from them. Enslaved people and freed Black people could not hold or own firearms. Slaveowners were allowed to inflict harsher and stricter punishments on their slaves.

Restrictions to stop Black people from gathering were not successful, especially as the population of enslaved people continued to grow. By 1741, New York City had twenty-one thousand residents, of which two thousand were Black. Fear and suspicions of others contributed to the New York Slave Insurrection of 1741, which is also referred to as the Great Negro Plot or the Conspiracy of 1741. Regardless of which heading or name is used, the premise of the event was the belief by some White New Yorkers that enslaved Black people and indentured and poor multiracial workers had plotted together to overthrow the city's government and take over New York.

Records of events often contradict each other. However, there is evidence that a number of fires happened in the city beginning in March. The first fire occurred at Fort George, which decimated the fort. During the next week, Lieutenant Governor George Clarke's house was engulfed in flames. Over the next few weeks, fires burned at least five more houses. New Yorkers began attributing the fires to arsonists, which fed into the fears of a plot.

When government leaders began their investigation into the causes of the fires, generous rewards were offered for information. Pardons were also available for people who provided the names of the participants. Accusations and rumors increased in number and complexity.

One of the key figures in the investigation was Mary Burton. Burton was a sixteen-year-old White indentured servant. She worked in John Hughson's tavern in New York City. On April 21st, 1741, Burton was made to testify before the jury. For her testimony, she was promised freedom and one hundred pounds. Burton stated that her boss, John Hughson, was one of the leaders of the conspiracy to destroy the city and kill the White residents.

Burton further stipulated that Hughson's wife, Sarah, along with three slaves named Caesar, Prince, and Cuffee, plotted with the tavern owner. Burton also connected Peggy Kerry, a White prostitute, to the plan. Burton claimed that Kerry, who was pregnant, perhaps with Ceasar's child, met with the group in the tavern to create the plans. Kerry was then compelled to testify and name others.

Though all six denied the allegations made by Burton, they were hanged.

Throughout the summer, Mary Burton continued her testimony. By the end of her time on the witness stand, her accusations resulted in the deaths of more than thirty slaves. When Burton started stating the names of leading citizens in New York City, she was no longer asked to testify.

Burton's and the forced testimony of others led to more than 150 people being arrested. They either testified against others or were compelled to confess to acts they had not performed. At least seventy enslaved people were deported because of accusations made against them.

The last person hanged as part of the alleged conspiracy was John Ury. In August 1741, Ury was found guilty of participating in the conspiracy. Though he had a number of people testify on behalf of his innocence, he was still executed. Charges were brought against the White schoolteacher for lying about being a Catholic priest. Though Burton asserted that Ury was a priest, he was not a Catholic priest.

For her time and testimony, Mary Burton was freed from her obligations as an indentured servant. She accepted her reward of one hundred pounds. In addition, the New York City Council sent a note to

Burton thanking her for her service. Once she had received her reward, Mary Burton promptly left the city.

Chapter 4 – Battling for New York City and a New Nation

Still a British colony in 1764, New York City was impacted by the Sugar Act passed by England. Great Britain was attempting to recoup the expenses incurred during the French and Indian War. This conflict was fought in North America between 1754 and 1763. England asserted that the colonies benefited greatly from its victory in the war. Known as a theater of the Seven Years' War, it resulted in the removal of the French from the colonies.

Molasses imported into the colonies were taxed as part of the Sugar Act. Though colonists did not want to pay the fees, the new duty was met with minimal resistance in the colonies. Most believed that Britain had the right to tax imported goods as part of trade duties. These types of taxes were imposed on everyone who lived in the British Empire.

However, the Stamp Act, which was approved by the British government in February 1765, incited the colonists to act. The difference between the reaction to the two acts was that the Stamp Act was perceived as an internal tax placed on just the colonists and not the entire empire. Colonists did not believe that King George III or the British Parliament had the right to tax them without representation.

In response to the perceived overreach of the British Parliament, the first group of the Sons of Liberty was formed in the summer of 1765. It is believed that Boston was home to the first chapter of the Sons of Liberty or Liberty Boys, but New York City quickly followed with the establishment of its own group.

Group members were united in their opposition to the growing interference of Great Britain in their lives. Local chapters of the Sons of Liberty met secretly; New York City's members gathered at Fraunces Tavern. In their meetings, members devised methods to disrupt the oppressive policies of the king and Parliament. There were coordinated boycotts and plans to harass the officials who were charged with collecting the revenue from the act. Encounters between tax collectors and the Sons of Liberty sometimes turned violent.

Isaac Sears, Marinus Willett, John Lamb, Alexander McDougall, and Hercules Mulligan helped form the New York City chapter of the Sons of Liberty. These men came from a variety of backgrounds. During the day, they worked in their known occupations as laborers, merchants, and artisans. They often dealt directly with British officials. In their secret Sons of Liberty meetings, the men risked their professions, family, and freedom to effect change in the colonies.

One of the many outcomes that resulted from the actions of the Sons of Liberty was the formation of the Stamp Act Congress. Nine of the thirteen colonies sent representatives to the meeting in New York City. Their goal was to develop a unified response opposing the Stamp Act. Delegates first met on October 7th, 1765, in Federal Hall.

Drawing of Federal Hall.
https://commons.wikimedia.org/wiki/File:Federal_Hall-Archibald_Robertson.jpg

The representatives agreed that Parliament had the right to regulate trade. However, they also stated that they did not believe the king and his government had the legal right or authority to tax the colonies. Since the colonists did not have any elected representatives in Parliament, that governing body could not impose taxes without agreement from the colonists.

By approving the Declaration of Rights and Grievances, the Stamp Act Congress asserted that the colonists were entitled to the same rights and liberties as those living in England. Therefore, similar to their British counterparts, American colonists were entitled to representation. Since England was so far away, the Stamp Act Congress stated that the colonists should be represented locally. Only those officials had the authority to impose internal taxes on the colonists.

In addition to declaring there could be no taxation without representation, the Stamp Act Congress affirmed its belief in the right to a trial by jury, just like other British subjects. The Stamp Act Congress professed its allegiance to and support of the king and his Parliament as part of the Declaration of Rights and Grievances.

Parliament and the British king denied all claims and arguments detailed by the Stamp Act Congress. The British government reasserted its belief in its control over the colonies. It did not recognize the Stamp Act Congress as a legitimate representative body.

Britain continued with its steps, implementing a tax on legal documents, newspapers, informational pamphlets, playing cards, and broadsides. These papers needed a stamp fastened to them as a means of showing the tax had been paid. The Stamp Act took effect on November 1st, 1765.

The British ship HMS *Edward*, laden with official Stamp Act stamps, arrived in New York Harbor on October 22nd, 1765. The ship was greeted by a crowd of over two thousand protesters, who were led by the Sons of Liberty. The crowd prevented the ship from docking, but the stamps were covertly offloaded and stored at Fort George two days after the HMS *Edward* arrived in New York City. New York's Lieutenant Governor Cadwallader Colden stationed additional troops at the fort to protect the stamps.

Painting of Lieutenant Governor Colden.

On the eve of the enactment of the Stamp Act, New York City's Sons of Liberty met at Burn's City Arms Tavern, which was located at the intersection of Broadway and Thames, to organize their next steps. They organized a funeral procession due to the death of liberty. The protesters marched from the Common, which is now City Hall Park, along Broadway until the protesters reached Fort George. During the peaceful march, the group chanted, "Liberty!"

The Sons of Liberty also agreed they would no longer import goods and merchandise from England. Beginning on January 1ˢᵗ, 1766, the rebellious group sought support from city merchants to cease the sale of any goods from Britain.

Colden, the lieutenant governor of New York, who was acting governor during this protest, continued to publicly support the Stamp

Act. In addition to increasing the troop numbers at Fort George, Colden ordered the reorientation of the cannons. Instead of facing toward the harbor to protect the city, the cannons were turned toward the city.

Again, the Sons of Liberty reacted. They delivered a threatening letter to Colden. Over the next four days, mobs protested throughout the city. Referred to as the General Terror, from November 1st to the 4th, groups dragged Colden's effigy and created mayhem in the streets of New York City. They lit effigies near Fort George, threatened the lives of British officials, and threw bricks and stones at British encampments.

Their actions caused the acting governor to state that he would not take any more actions to implement the Stamp Act. Any further steps to enforce the act would be made when the new governor arrived from England.

New York City's Sons of Liberty were effective in their organized protests against the Stamp Act. Eventually, the Stamp Act was repealed by Parliament in March 1766.

On King George III's birthday, New York City celebrated Parliament's reversal of the Stamp Act. The Sons of Liberty constructed New York City's first liberty pole near the location of the barracks for the British troops. Liberty poles were often topped with a flag or liberty cap. Liberty caps were based on red head coverings donned by freed slaves over two thousand years ago, and they became a symbol of those supporting the revolution. It is believed that Samuel Adams embraced the red caps with the words "liberty" or "liberty or death" woven on them as an emblem for the revolution. Colonists erected the poles as a symbol of their desire for freedom or liberty from the king and Parliament. From June 4th, 1766, until January 1770, New York City's liberty pole was destroyed at least four times by British troops and rebuilt by the Sons of Liberty.

The barracks themselves became a point of contention between New York City colonists and the British. In 1765, Parliament passed the Quartering Act. This law compelled local legislatures to pay for some of the expenses to house British troops. Many colonists did not believe that soldiers were necessary in the colonies; therefore, this act was just another means to tax them.

When British troops were posted in New York City in 1766, New York's Assembly denied England's demand for money for the troops. In response, Parliament agreed to a new law, the New York Restraining

Act. Under this act, New York could no longer vote on or pass any new laws until the people followed the requirements of the Quartering Act.

Finally, in December 1769, New York conceded and paid an insultingly small amount to support the troops. Angered, the British troops tried unsuccessfully to chop down the liberty pole. Two days later, on January 15th, 1770, the British soldiers used gunpowder to divide the pole. Throughout the night, they cut the pole into pieces. At one of the meeting places of the Sons of Liberty, Montayne's Tavern, the soldiers stacked the wood on the tavern's front stoop. The troops then hung taunting handbills intended to insult the Sons of Liberty.

The leaders of the defiant group, Walter Quackenbos and Isaac Sears, captured two of the soldiers. They marched the soldiers to the office of the mayor, insisting they be arrested. In the meantime, more colonists gathered at the mayor's office, as did reinforcements from the barracks.

The British troops were sent back to their barracks by the mayor, but they were followed by the angry colonists. When they reached the top of Golden Hill, the colonists surrounded the soldiers. Another group of soldiers arrived, and they were able to assist the group that had been surrounded. British soldiers used their bayonets and wounded some colonists. A riot ensued. Some say the first blood of the American Revolution was shed in the Battle of Golden Hill in January 1770. This occurred two months before the Boston massacre.

Parliament's passing of the Tea Act in 1773 created the tipping point in the confrontations between the British and the Sons of Liberty. The British East India Company was given a monopoly on the sales of tea in the colonies. Parliament did this to assist the company in managing its debt. It was also supposed to help curb smuggling. However, in reality, for the colonists, the East India Company, which sold much more than tea, could now control the flow of and cost of goods sold in the colonies. In essence, the Tea Act added more cost burdens, or the equivalent of taxes, on these goods.

The New York chapter of the Sons of Liberty responded by creating the Committee of Vigilance. This committee was charged with ensuring that no shipments of tea from the British East India Company were permitted into New York Harbor. The Sons of Liberty organized a petition against the importation of tea, which more than two hundred New York businessmen, merchants, artisans, and others signed. The petition stated that anyone who was knowingly involved with the British East India Company and its tea was their enemy and against liberty. More than three thousand New Yorkers protested the Tea Act and the East India Company on the steps of city hall in December 1773.

Also occurring that same month was the well-known Boston Tea Party. Colonists dressed as Native Americans tossed chests full of tea from three different ships into the harbor. Word of this action was delivered to the New York Sons of Liberty by Paul Revere shortly after the incident.

In support of their Bostonian brethren, the New York Sons of Liberty formed their own chapter. Led by Alexander McDougall, this group would perform similar acts of resistance against the British authorities. New York's lesser-known tea party occurred in April 1774. The *Nancy*, a British ship, arrived in New York Harbor loaded with almost seven hundred chests filled with tea. Her cargo of tea was more than double the amount involved in the Boston Tea Party.

A letter was delivered to Captain Benjamin Lockyer from the Sons of Liberty. They offered Lockyer the choice of returning to England with his cargo and the ship intact, or the Sons of Liberty would board the *Nancy*, and Lockyer would lose his life. The captain agreed to sail back to England with the British East India Company's tea. Members of the Sons of Liberty escorted Lockyer through the city so he could procure the goods needed for his return trip.

A few days later, the *London* reached New York Harbor. The Sons of Liberty received word from their Philadelphia counterparts that the ship had chests of tea aboard. The captain, Chambers, kept his own private supply of eighteen chests of tea. That was a sufficient enough quantity for the Sons of Liberty to capture the captain, raid the ship, and toss the tea into the harbor.

The empty chests were set ablaze in the streets of the city. Chambers escaped from capture and boarded the *Nancy* to return trip to England.

Protests against British rule and King George III continued in New York City until the start of the American Revolution. On July 9th, 1776, the Declaration of Independence was read at City Hall Park. Members of the Continental Army and George Washington were in attendance for the reading.

Inspired by the words of the Declaration of Independence, the crowd, led by Isaac Sears and other members of the Sons of Liberty, paraded through the streets of the city. As they progressed, they became violent. Loyalists' homes were vandalized by the unruly crowd, smashing windows and breaking other items.[1]

When the mob arrived at Bowling Green Park, they worked together to destroy the four-thousand-pound statue of King George III. Legend says the statue was chopped into pieces and transported to Connecticut. At a factory, the pieces were melted and reformed as musket balls to be used in the fighting against the British.

Painting of the mob pulling down the statue of George III at Bowling Green.
https://commons.wikimedia.org/wiki/File:William_Walcutt_statue_George_III.png

The first significant battle of the war after the signing of the Declaration of Independence was the Battle of Brooklyn, also called the Battle of Long Island. This battle for control of New York City was fought in August 1776.

General William Howe was the commanding officer of the British forces. He theorized that if the British could control the Hudson River and New York City, they would be able to separate the colonies. Once the colonies were geographically divided, it would be easier for the British to gain a foothold in the area.

George Washington arrived in New York City before Howe. He divided his troops between Manhattan and Brooklyn in a defensive

---

[1] Loyalist is a term used to describe those who remained loyal to the British Crown. A Redcoat refers to a British soldier. A Patriot is someone who fought for independence.

posture. However, these positions did not provide a means to replace troops as the battle progressed, nor did Washington set up a route to evade capture by Howe's troops. The most significant issue for the Patriots was the gap in coverage in their line. At the top of Guan Heights, there were not enough soldiers to protect the Jamaica Pass.

There were three roads that led to the Patriots' position atop Guan Heights, so Howe created three lines of men to attack. Just after midnight on August 27th, Howe sent two lines forward, and the rebels responded. Then, the Redcoats moved their third line of soldiers to surprise the Patriots by approaching from the rear, the gap in the Patriots' line.

Major General Putnam was compelled to move his forces, which had been stationed on Long Island's Brooklyn Heights, after Howe marched his columns forward on August 27th. Meanwhile, the main British attack swung right and, finding the road undefended, attacked the American rear.

Now, the rebels were surrounded and outnumbered by the British. Instead of proceeding and executing a decisive attack, Howe took two days to prepare his final assault on Washington and his troops. George Washington took full advantage of the pause in fighting. During the night of August 29th, Washington moved his men across the East River to escape.

Though the Patriots were defeated in the Battle of Brooklyn, Washington's maneuver saved his army from being captured by the British, which allowed them to continue to fight. England controlled New York City for the duration of the war.

Washington recognized his need for better information about the enemy's troops, movements, and location. An experienced soldier and leader of the newly formed Rangers, Lieutenant Colonel Thomas Knowlton provided Washington with the intelligence-gathering skills needed.

Knowlton's Rangers were tasked with acquiring information about the British troops in September 1776 in preparation for the Battle of Harlem Heights. Now considered the "father of American military intelligence," Knowlton sought a volunteer who was willing to go behind enemy lines in pursuit of information. Nathan Hale accepted the mission.

Attired as a schoolmaster, the twenty-one-year-old Hale traversed from Harlem Heights, where the Continual Army camped, and entered enemy territory. On September 21st, 1776, Nathan Hale was captured by the British forces. General Howe ordered Hale's execution for the following day on Manhattan Island.

Drawing of the hanging of Nathan Hale.
https://commons.wikimedia.org/wiki/File:Memories_of_the_Union_-_execution_of_Nathan_Hale_on_the_site_of_east_Broadway,_corner_of_Market_Street,_New_York,_September_21,_1776_-_M._Nevin._LCCN2006691565.jpg

Knowing that he was about to die in the morning, Hale sent his report on British troop movements back to Knowlton before his execution. Accounts of Hale's hanging were reported in the diaries of British officers who witnessed it. They stated that Hale was composed as they strung him up. Before he died, Hale said, "I only regret that I have but one life to lose for my country." Nathan Hale was hanged on September 22nd, 1776, in Manhattan.

From a military stance, the Battle of Harlem Heights was a draw. However, for the fledgling American troops, the battle boosted their morale.

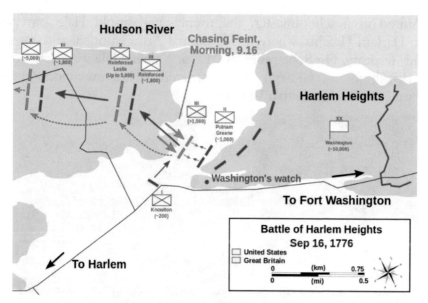

Map of the Battle of Harlem Heights.

Seven years later, a triumphant General George Washington and Governor George Clinton led American soldiers into New York City. The British occupation of the city and the American Revolution ended. The Paris Peace Treaty of 1783 officially concluded the American War of Independence. A new capital and a new nation emerged from the fighting.

Chapter 5 – From the New Capital to Leading City

The Articles of Confederation stipulated that New York City would serve as the temporary capital of the new country. Beginning in 1785, Congress convened in New York's City Hall. Located at 26 Wall Street, the US federal government emerged from meetings held in this building. Congressional sessions were held here until 1790. The building was renamed Federal Hall.

On March 4th, 1789, George Washington was unanimously elected as the first president of the new country by Congress. Washington was sworn in as the president of the new republic the following month on April 30th on the balcony of Federal Hall.

While located in New York City, Congress passed milestone laws that continue to govern the United States today. Some of the legacy bills passed by Congress in its early years included the Bill of Rights; these are the first ten amendments to the Constitution. Laws were voted on and approved to establish the Department of the Treasury, the State Department, the Justice Department, and the War Department. Before the capital was relocated, Congress also formed the Supreme Court and the federal court system with the passage of the Judiciary Act in 1789.

Deciding on the permanent location of the nation's capital city was a difficult decision for Congress. After much haggling, bickering, and compromising, a deal was negotiated. Now referred to as the Dinner Party Compromise of 1790, Thomas Jefferson, Alexander Hamilton, and James Madison supported an agreement to relocate the capital to the shores of the Potomac River. While the area and buildings were being constructed, the capital would be moved to Philadelphia.

The first secretary of the treasury, Alexander Hamilton, had a vision for the new nation's economy. His ideas benefited New York. His astute fiscal dealings provided New York with a new path to lead the country as its financial leader. Part of the Dinner Party Compromise ensured that New York's debt incurred during the Revolutionary War would be forgiven.

Further solidifying New York's role as a leading city was the Buttonwood Agreement of 1792. Before this contract, merchants and traders had informally brokered deals on Wall Street. However, the financial Panic of 1792 created concern among legitimate traders and speculators. Deceitful investors caused brokers to become leery of trading.

To reestablish trust in trading under the buttonwood tree, a group of twenty-four merchants and brokers agreed to trade only with each other. This deal, signed on Wall Street, formed the new country's stock exchange. Its purpose was to ensure that the public would have confidence in the legitimacy of trades and deals brokered on 68 Wall Street.

An outgrowth of the Buttonwood Agreement was the formalization of the New York Stock Exchange (NYSE) in 1817. The NYSE also created a physical location for the new organization by renting rooms at 40 Wall Street.

As New York City entered into the 19th century, it did so as the largest city in the country, with a burgeoning population of nearly 100,000 residents. Concerns were mounting about how the city would be able to safely grow and accommodate all its residents. The city's inhabitants tripled in the years immediately after the American Revolution. This dramatic increase in population and the city's inability to determine the best way to develop and sell tracts of land between 14th Street and Washington Heights prompted New York City Council to seek assistance.

The New York State Legislature convened a three-member commission on April 3rd, 1807. The three members were Gouverneur Morris (one of the Founding Fathers), former Senator John Rutherfurd, and New York State's Surveyor General Simeon DeWitt. The commission was charged with developing a plan for the eventual northward expansion of the city.

DeWitt's apprentice, twenty-year-old John Randel Jr., was the chief surveyor for the project. For two years, Randel surveyed the eleven-thousand-acre island. To attain precise measurements, Randel is credited with inventing a number of surveying tools. His field notes filled forty leather-bound notebooks. Randel's completed surveys were detailed on three hand-drawn documents that were almost nine feet in length.

On March 22nd, 1811, Mayor DeWitt Clinton and other New York City officials accepted the plan. Not all New Yorkers supported the changes, but the plan was enacted nevertheless. Key features of the design included new streets being constructed from east to west and avenues fashioned to flow north to south. Eleven of the avenues and 155 of the streets created in the plan are still part of New York City's grid system today.

As part of the commission's grid plan, only 470 acres were set aside for open space and parks. That situation was rectified later in the century with the formation of Central Park.

The largest city in the nation also earned other monikers. One of its first nicknames was published in 1807 in *Salmagundi*, which was a satirical magazine created by author Washington Irving; his brother, William; and another author, James Kirke Paulding. In a periodical, the trio lampooned the way of life, people, and politics found in New York City.

Irving's version of New York City is called Gotham, which is based on a medieval village. The inhabitants of the village from long ago were goat herders who lacked common sense and good judgment. To avoid having to pay to have a road paved for the king, the villagers all acted crazy. The king bypassed the village on his travels. Irving's parallels between the two showed New Yorkers as self-absorbed, irrational people. Certainly, Gotham, with its connection to Batman, holds a much different aura!

Irving also devised a term for native New Yorkers—Knickerbockers. In his *A History of New York: From the Beginning of the World to the End of the Dutch Dynasty*, Irving's narrator is Diedrich Knickerbocker. In this tale, Irving mocks New Yorkers' lack of knowledge about their own history. The term "Knickerbocker" refers to the first European settlers in New York, the Dutch. The pants worn in the 1600s by the Dutch settlers sat just below one's kneecap. So, a Knickerbocker was one whose lineage could be traced to the Dutch settlers.

The city earned many nicknames. The city also witnessed a massive project that had a major impact on its continued growth and economy. Clinton's Big Ditch, or the Erie Canal, quadrupled New York City's population in the three decades after the canal opened.

Also known as Clinton's Folly, the canal was proposed and propelled into reality with the backing of DeWitt Clinton. As New York City's mayor and then as the state's governor, Clinton pursued the funding for the massive project. Spanning 363 miles, the Erie Canal took from 1817 to 1825 to complete.

The federal government did not believe the project was doable and would not supply any funding. Naysayers considered the distance, terrain, lack of technology and engineering, and costs to be prohibitive.

However, Clinton's vision of linking Lake Erie with the Hudson River was completed and considered an engineering masterpiece. Once the Erie Canal was finished, it became the longest canal in the Western Hemisphere.

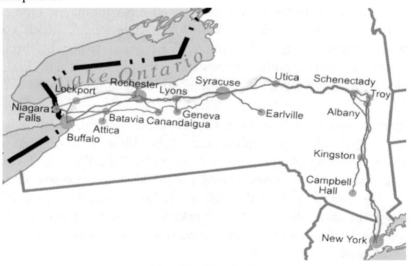

Map of the Erie Canal.

The canal was constructed with the manpower of many immigrants and horses, and it was deemed a success on opening day. Freight costs were drastically reduced. Before the canal, the fee to ship a ton of freight from New York City to Buffalo was $100. That same ton of freight shipped on the Erie Canal cost only $6 to transport. Construction costs for the canal totaled around $7 million. After the Erie Canal operated for just three years, it had collected enough in tolls that the construction costs plus interest were paid.

New York City's prominence as a commercial and financial center extended beyond the United States with the opening of the Erie Canal. New York harbors processed more goods and ships than Baltimore, New Orleans, and Boston combined.

With its population growing and its expanding role in industry, living conditions in New York became a concern. The grid layout that had been utilized to organize the development of the city did not include large open spaces and parks for the increasing influx of residents.

One proponent who urged the city to establish a park for its citizens was the editor of the *New York Evening Post*, William Cullen Bryant. In his role as editor of a city paper and as an internationally acclaimed poet, he used his column to bring attention to the need for a park. He encouraged the elite New Yorkers to support a park so that the city could equal the grandeur of European cities and their extensive gardens and parks. Additionally, Bryant wanted the parks to be accessible for all city dwellers, not just the upper class.

Support for a park grew in the city and in the state legislature. Funding to purchase land for Central Park was approved in 1853. Land located between 59th Street and 106th Street and from Fifth to Eighth Avenue was acquired for around five million dollars.

However, not all of the land was available for sale. New York City utilized its power of eminent domain to force the relocation of those living on the over eight hundred acres that the city obtained for the park. It is estimated that almost 1,600 residents were displaced to make room for the park.

Included in this acreage was a small section called Seneca Village. This area of housing resulted from the partition of John and Elizabeth Whitehead's farmland. In 1825, the couple divided their farm into two hundred lots. Andrew Williams, a Black shoe shiner and member of the New York African Society for Mutual Relief, bought the first three lots from the Whiteheads for $125. The society sought to assist Black families with housing options in the city.

Epiphany Davis, a store clerk, joined Williams as a Black landowner when he purchased twelve lots. After the African Methodist Episcopal (AME) Zion Church bought six lots to build a new church, more Black families bought land from the Whiteheads. One hundred of the two hundred lots were sold to Black people. Many of the other pieces of land were sold to Irish immigrants, another group that many did not want in their neighborhood.

Black males who owned land valued at $250 and who had been residents of New York State for three years were eligible to vote. White males did not need to meet either qualifier before they were permitted to vote. New York City had only seventy-one Black males who owned property in 1850. Twenty percent of Black males who met the voting requirements in New York City owned homes in Seneca Village.

When New York City sought the land for Central Park, there were about 350 residents in Seneca Village. Almost 70 percent were free Blacks; the other third were mainly Irish immigrants. The village had grown to have cemeteries, three churches—African Union, AME Zion, and All Angels—and its own school. Half of the residents owned their own homes in the village.

In 1857, the city forced all the residents to leave their homes. They were paid $700 for each lot of land that they owned. Residents felt this was well below the actual value of the land. Some people tried to sue the city, but nothing came of it. The families from Seneca Village were dispersed throughout the city.

Once the city had the land, it needed a plan to transform the acreage acquired into a grand park. The Central Park Commissioners hosted a design contest. The Greensward Plan created by Frederick Law Olmsted and Calvert Vaux was selected as the winning entry from the thirty-three entries that the commission received.

Their design created a bucolic sanctuary in the midst of New York City's urban landscape. To maintain the pastoral setting, crosstown traffic was obscured on roadways that were situated below park level. Eleven overpasses were constructed over the transverse thoroughfares. The thirty-six arches and bridges were designed to blend into the landscape. Pedestrian and carriage traffic were separated when forming the park.

Many Irish and German immigrants provided the labor to construct the park. They toiled for ten hours a day for one dollar. Other craftsmen earned more for their labor. Over ten thousand workers were needed throughout the entire construction project. Almost five million cubic yards of earthen materials were moved to create the new topography of the park. A drainage system that traveled through ninety-five miles of underground piping was dug by hand. More than five million shrubs, trees, and vegetation were planted.

In 1858, the Lake was the first section of Central Park that was opened to the public. Construction continued for the next fifteen years. The total cost to construct the park exceeded fourteen million dollars, which was well over the design estimate of one and a half million dollars.

In 1853, the same year that funding was approved for Central Park, New York City hosted America's first world fair. Emulating London's Great Exhibition in 1851, the Exhibition of the Works of Industry of All Nations was intended to showcase America and its talents. To house the exhibition, the Crystal Palace was constructed on land that is today's Bryant Park.

Conceived and designed by architects Charles Gildemeister and Georg J. Carstensen, the Crystal Palace was a stunning exhibition hall. At the time of its use and construction, the building was the largest building in the Western Hemisphere. Shaped like a Greek cross, this technological marvel extended an entire city block. A 100-foot glass dome capped the 150-foot-tall cast iron and steel structure. The building was as impressive as the wonders that it held.

The Latting Observatory also opened as part of the exhibition. Reaching 315 feet, the wooden edifice was constructed with three landings at 125 feet, 225 feet, and 300 feet. On each of the landings, visitors could view all-encompassing scenes of New Jersey, Lower Manhattan, Staten Island, and Queens. These breathtaking vistas were said to have inspired Gustave Eiffel's tower for the 1889 Paris World's Fair, known today as the Eiffel Tower.

The exhibition drew in over one million visitors, including newly sworn-in President Franklin Pierce. He gave a speech to commemorate the achievements that the fair highlighted in its displays. A set of porcelain shown by Haughwout and Dailey at the fair caught the president's attention and was purchased for his White House china service.

"Song of the Exhibition" by Walt Whitman was inspired by the exposition and the Crystal Palace.

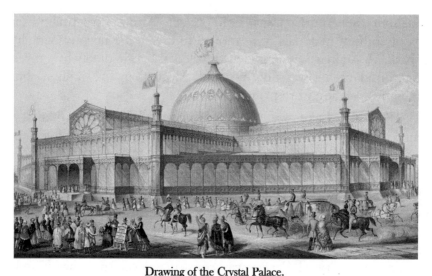

Drawing of the Crystal Palace.

Items and inventions shown in the exhibition displayed the technological advances of the time period. Elisha Otis revealed his new innovation to awe-struck crowds: a safe passenger elevator. With great flair, Otis showed the skeptical audiences the safety feature that made his lift safe. Otis stood on the elevator floor while it rose up. Then, he had the cable lines that secured the platform cut. To the crowd's astonishment, the elevator platform that he stood on did not descend downward. Otis's elevator design included a brake that safely held the platform.

Now that the public's concerns about the safety of elevators were assuaged, Otis's orders for his invention increased dramatically. His first installation of a passenger elevator occurred in New York City in 1857 at E. V. Haughwout and Company's department store. The spectacular growth of the New York City skyline was now possible with Otis elevators.

Another lasting invention that was showcased at the Crystal Palace was the Steinway piano. Henry Steinway's piano performance won first place at the exhibition, which established the quality of his new Manhattan workshop.

Many visitors viewed their first photograph as they toured the exhibitions. Mathew Brady's picture of Admiral Matthew Perry was on display. Samuel Morse's telegraph was shown fully operating in the Crystal Palace. Singer sewing machines and more were presented to visitors during the exhibition.

Both buildings were short-lived. The Latting Observatory was destroyed by a fire that originated in a neighboring cooper's shop in 1856. Two years later, the Crystal Palace succumbed to a fire of unknown origins.

New York City continued to grow and prosper. Cultural venues were added to the city. In 1854, the city's newest opera house, the Academy of Music, opened its doors. With the largest stage in the world at the time, the opening performance was Bellini's *Norma*. Though its size was impressive, with seating available for over four thousand, it did not contain enough quality seats for the expanding upper class of the city.

Academy of Music.
https://commons.wikimedia.org/wiki/File:Academy_of_Music_(New_York_City)_crop.jpg

Attending the opera was a sign of social status. Old money families were able to purchase family boxes at the Academy of Music. The Stuyvesant, Beekman, Belmont, and Astor families had subscription seats for the opera performances at East 14th Street and Irving Place.

However, the up-and-coming new money millionaires were left seatless. Allegedly, William Henry Vanderbilt was willing to pay $30,000 for an opera box for a season's worth of performances, and his money was refused. Not to be outdone, the newly rich began their plans to open the Metropolitan Opera House. The competition eventually closed the doors of the Academy of Music.

Chapter 6– Turning Points

There was a division growing between new and old money, and the gap between those with money and those without money was expanding. One of New York City's new millionaires and one of the richest men in the world, Peter Cooper, sought to share his success with others.

Growing up, Cooper only attended school for one year. However, his innate curiosity and work ethic paved the road to earning millions. His money was earned through a variety of ventures that involved the iron and steel industry, real estate, and telecommunications. Not only did Cooper make money from his investments, but he was also a successful inventor. He found a more efficient method to tow canal boats, the first locomotive steam engine ("Tom Thumb"), the process to manufacture gelatin, and much more.

One of the ways he shared his wealth and provided opportunities for others to pursue their talents was to open his own school. In 1859, he founded the Cooper Union for the Advancement of Science and Art, which was located at Astor Place. The building in which he housed his school was also the first building with fireproof iron I-beams, which Cooper invented and produced. Another first for the building was that Cooper built it with space for an elevator. An elevator designed by Elisha Otis eventually filled the shaft.

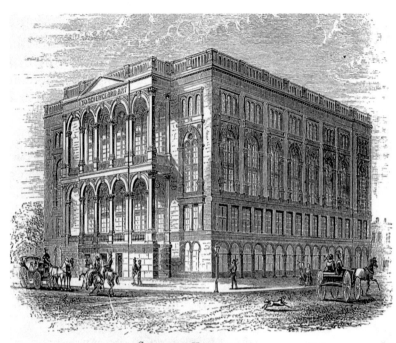

COOPER UNION.

Cooper Union.

https://commons.wikimedia.org/wiki/File:Cooper_Union_from_Miller%27s_New_York_as_it_is_(14596084839).jpg

The building was remarkable, and Cooper's philosophies about its use were also revolutionary. He envisioned a school that merged the sciences and the arts. Anyone who had a desire to learn and pledged to excel was welcome to earn an education. Admission to the school was not based on social or economic class, gender, or skin color. Cooper Union was tuition-free for members of the working class.

Cooper understood that many people were interested in learning but could not attend school as full-time students, so he added a public reading room. Anyone was welcome to read the most current newspapers and periodicals for free. The reading room was open until 10:00 p.m. and was accessible to those who worked all day. Classes at the school were also offered in the evening to meet the needs of the working class.

Records show that more than three thousand people a week utilized the reading room. One was a future Supreme Court justice, Felix Frankfurter. Thomas Edison's only formalized schooling was the chemistry classes that he attended at Cooper Union.

Cooper envisioned his school to have a broader impact than free tuition and a reading room. As a member of New York City's Board of Aldermen, Cooper wanted a secular space in the city where people could engage in discussions about politics and culture. Therefore, he established the Great Hall, which was located in the basement of the school's Foundation Building. At the time of its construction, the Great Hall had the largest secular seating capacity in the city.

Abraham Lincoln, who was not yet a declared candidate for the presidency, was invited to speak by a New York City Republican group. Lincoln delivered a pivotal speech in February 1860. A view held by many, including Lincoln, is that this speech and its impact helped Lincoln secure the Republican nomination for the presidency.

At over seven thousand words, the Cooper Union speech was Lincoln's longest. In the speech, Lincoln articulated his views on slavery, stating that Congress was morally obligated to stop the spread of slavery. He also shared his thoughts on the importance of the Union. The speech was printed in the city's newspapers on the following day, which quickly garnered Lincoln support from many in the city and nation.

Not only did this emotionally charged speech in New York City help elect Lincoln as the country's sixteenth president, but a Mathew Brady portrait also became an iconic image of the future president. Lincoln wore a new silk top hat that he had purchased on Broadway. Brady's photograph became the image used on many of Lincoln's campaign materials.

Soon after Lincoln was elected president, the country became embroiled in the Civil War. The American Civil War began in 1861. By 1863, the fighting had taken a toll on the Union forces, and the flow of volunteers greatly diminished. To address the shortage of troops, Congress passed the Conscription or Enrollment Act.

The law stipulated that able-bodied White males needed to register for the military. Additional qualifiers stated that all White males between twenty and thirty-five and unmarried White males between thirty-five and forty-five were subject to service in the Union Army.

However, there were two ways that an eligible male could avoid military service. A payment of three hundred dollars to the federal government would buy one's way out of fighting, or a draftee could hire someone else to fight for them.

Though many Northerners supported Lincoln and the Union, many did not support the Conscription Act. Workers' earnings were often less than five hundred dollars annually. Therefore, the working class viewed the draft as unfair since rich White males could afford to pay the fee not to fight. Adding to the discontent and anger of poorer White laborers was the fact that this act did not include Black men. Since they were not viewed as citizens, Black men did not have to sign up for the military draft.

Negative responses to the law caused riots in cities like Boston and Detroit. New York City's first draft was held in July 1863. The reaction to the lottery resulted in four days of violence in the city. These riots are known as the New York City draft riots of 1863.

Thousands of rioters swarmed the streets of the city. Consisting mostly of foreign-born residents, especially Irish immigrants, the angry mobs caused more than $1.5 million in damage to structures in the city. Targeted buildings included the city's draft headquarters, but other buildings and homes were also affected.

Though the catalyst for the riots was the lottery for the draft, underlying tensions between rich and poor, races, and the struggle for jobs added to the outpouring of anger and violence. As the riots continued, rioters attacked the homes of the rich, Black-owned businesses and residences, and abolitionists.

Rioters even set the Colored Orphan Asylum on fire. The children were not physically harmed in the attack. They were relocated to the city's almshouse.

Four thousand Union troops, men who had just fought in the Battle of Gettysburg, were called upon to quell the riot.

Estimates of the number of people who died because of the riots range from two hundred to two thousand. Thousands were injured. It remains the deadliest riot in the history of America.

The riots dramatically impacted the African Americans living in the city. Twenty-five percent of Black city residents were left homeless due to the damage to their homes. Thousands of Black people left the city after the rioting. Protests from neighboring property owners prevented the rebuilding of the Colored Orphan Asylum in the same location. It was eventually built in today's Harlem.

On August 19th, 1863, the lottery for the military draft was reinstated without any issues.

Twenty months later, the city celebrated the end of the Civil War. However, the people's celebration quickly turned to sorrow two days later when President Lincoln was assassinated. Lincoln's funeral entourage was greeted by more than 500,000 as it passed through New York City on its way to Illinois.

Neither the Civil War nor the draft riots lessened the political strife or class divisions in New York City. An area of the city that clearly demonstrated the stratification of people was the infamous neighborhood of Five Points.

This neighborhood was named for the convergence of four streets that created an intersection with five corners. The original street names were Little Water, Orange, Anthony, and Cross. There had once been a five-acre lake, the Collect Pond, where Five Points was located. New York City's drinking water was provided through the spring-fed pond during the 1600s and 1700s.

As New York City's population continued to increase, businesses were pushed to different parts of the city. City regulations designated where noisy and dirty industries could be located. Tanneries and slaughterhouses were moved to the edges of Collect Pond. Over time, pollutants were discharged into the pond, making the water a health hazard.

Plans were developed to clean the water and banks of the pond. However, none of them were fully implemented. To remedy the problem of a toxic pond and the need for land for residential buildings, the pond was filled in with soil and earth from nearby construction projects.

A new neighborhood, Paradise Square, was erected on the area that had been Collect Pond. However, since the pond was spring-fed, there was still water flowing underneath the new neighborhood. The land never fully stabilized. Mosquitos and flooding became growing problems. Sections of buildings started to sink in the putrid marshlands. Muddy streets and fears of diseases from the insects and bugs prevalent in the swampland caused the original residents of Paradise Square to abandon the area.

Thus, Five Points became home to those who could not afford to live anywhere else in the city. Newly arrived immigrants and African Americans settled into housing that would become the city's first tenements. The area began earning a reputation for its horrific poverty, debauchery, and living conditions.

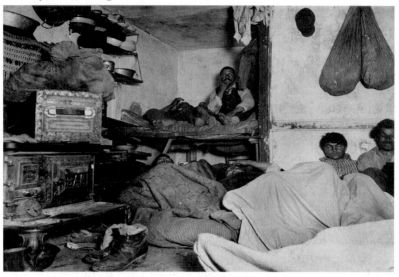

Crowded tenement.

Frontiersman and Creek War veteran Davy Crockett toured Five Points as a member of Congress. He claimed that he would prefer returning to battle than to go out in Five Points after dark. English author Charles Dickens, who lived and wrote about such situations, visited the area in 1841. He was appalled by the way people were living.

Even though the quality of life was dreadful for the residents of Five Points, more and more people were desperate to find housing and had no other option than to continue to move into the area. Due to the shortage of housing, landlords divided the apartments into additional units. Horse stables, attics, basements, and all other available spaces were converted into housing, adding to the overcrowded and squalid living conditions in Five Points.

More than half of the residents were Irish immigrants. German, Italian, and Chinese immigrants, along with African Americans, also lived in Five Points. Prejudices against immigrants, Black people, Jews, and Catholics made it difficult for many of the Five Points residents to find work that paid enough to move from the area. Children often had jobs to help their families eke out a living.

Three counties accounted for the majority of the Irish immigrants. Changes in the system of landownership in Ireland left many Irish farmers renting from British landlords instead of working for themselves. Subsistence farming left farmers and their families malnourished. Adding to their dire situation was the destruction of the potato crops from the blight.

Some Irish landlords began sending their tenant farmers to New York to eliminate having to deal with starving tenants. Inhumane conditions on the ships caused numerous deaths before their arrival in New York. Even with the horrors they escaped and what the immigrants endured in Five Points, life in the tenements was preferable to facing starvation at home.

The overcrowding in Five Points contributed to the violence and unsavory lifestyle of its residents. Murder, prostitution, street gangs, poverty, and disease were prominent in Five Points. Some of the more notable gangs that were prevalent included the Plug Uglies, Roach Guards, and Shirt Tails. The Protestant-based and anti-immigrant Bowery Boys often battled the newly arrived Irish Catholic Dead Rabbits over territory, politics, and power.

Painting of Five Points.
https://commons.wikimedia.org/wiki/File:The_Five_Points_MET_DP265419_altered.jpg

Political power and influence rose from the gangs and their control of Five Points and other parts of New York City. Immigrants living in Five

Points began to have a voice in politics through the powerful Tammany Hall. Originally formed in 1789, Tammany Hall was a charitable group that transformed into a political organization. In 1817, Irish immigrants were accepted into Tammany Hall.

Links between the gangs in Five Points and Tammany Hall were developed and facilitated through leaders like Boss William Tweed. A quid pro quo system that controlled Five Points and other impoverished areas of New York City was firmly established during Boss Tweed's reign.

For the struggling, newly arrived immigrants, social service agencies were not available to assist with transitioning to New York City. Tammany Hall provided that service. Ward bosses and their underlings would help immigrants find housing, jobs, and loans. In return, loyalty, often in the form of votes, was expected and most often received.

Gangs were compensated for their assistance in controlling the neighborhoods. Intimidation at the polls ensured that politicians Tammany Hall and Boss Tweed endorsed were elected. By 1860, Tweed controlled the mayor's office, New York's governor, and the state's speaker of the house.

Corruption ran rampant in the city, which supported Boss Tweed's lavish lifestyle. Eventually, Tweed's system of bribery and kickbacks was exposed, and he was arrested. It is estimated that anywhere between $20,000,000 and $200,000,000 were stolen by the Tweed Ring.

Political cartoons created by Thomas Nast contributed to Tweed's downfall. Nast drew his satirical works for *Harper's Weekly*. Using his cartoons as a vehicle to address the fraud and corruption of Tweed's control over Tammany Hall, Nast sought to expose Tweed and his cronies. The creation of over 140 cartoons that depicted Tweed in a negative light helped end his reign.

THE "BRAINS"

THAT ACHIEVED THE TAMMANY VICTORY AT THE ROCHESTER DEMOCRATIC CONVENTION.

One of Thomas Nast's cartoons of Boss Tweed.
https://commons.wikimedia.org/wiki/File:Nast-Boss-Tweed-1871.jpg

Even after Tweed sent his lawyer to intimidate and bribe Nast, the cartoonist continued his quest. Many of Nast's ideas complemented editorials and articles that were published in *The New York Times,* whose editor, Louis Jennings, also pursued the demise of Tweed and the Irish.

Their work came to fruition with the Orange Riots of 1871.

July 12th and the Battle of Boyne in 1690 is a significant date in Irish history. On that day, King William of Orange was victorious over King James II. Orangemen's Day commemorates the Protestant ascendancy in Ireland. In New York City, skirmishes between Irish Catholics and Protestants occurred during the 1870 recognition of the triumph of the Orangemen. Many were injured, and there were at least eight fatalities.

The Loyal Orange Order applied for a parade permit for the 1871 anniversary. This was met with protests from Irish Catholic groups that cited the violence of 1870 as an issue. The request for a parade permit was denied because of safety concerns. The denial had the support and encouragement of Boss Tweed, who didn't know if his people could control the potential riots.

Governor John Hoffman overrode the decision and said the parade should be permitted. Hoffman, a Tweed politician, wanted to run for president. He knew that separating himself from Tweed and his corruption would be needed for a successful bid. Also, many New Yorkers and the media felt the parade should be allowed. If the Orange Order was denied their request, the city was yielding to the Irish Catholic mob. By overriding Tweed and the city's mayor, another Tweed politician, Hoffman was seeking support from Tweed's adversaries.

Though additional National Guard troops were on duty the day of the parade, it soon dissolved into a deadly melee. Crowds of angry Irish Catholics attempted to prevent the Orangemen from matching onto Eighth Avenue. No one is sure how the violence began. However, it is believed that at least sixty died as part of the Orange Riots.

Orange Riots.
https://commons.wikimedia.org/wiki/File:Orange_Riot_1871_crop.jpg

More than twenty thousand Irish Catholics marched in the funeral processions. The dead were laid to rest in Calvary Cemetery in Queens. Governor Hoffman was hung in effigy.

One of the National Guard soldiers was Private Thomas Nast (the same Nast who created images of Boss Tweed). From his position, he was able to view the chaos. Nast captured the images from the deadly slaughter in his political cartoon, which was published the following week. His images depicted Boss Tweed, Tammany Hall, and the Irish Catholics as the ones responsible for the death and destruction.

Hastening Tweed's final fall from grace was Jimmy O'Brien. He had obtained records that showed many of Tweed's illegal transactions. O'Brien and Tweed had a disagreement, so O'Brien used the Tammany Riots (also known as the Orange Riots) as a time to share his documentation on Tweed with *The New York Times*. The paperwork that O'Brien had showed evidence of the many payoffs that Tweed and his associates paid. Fictitious contracts and records of business transactions were also provided.

Estimates of the scope of the pilfering were between $45 million and over $1 billion in today's money.

In 1873, Tweed was convicted on charges of larceny and fraud. After serving a year in prison, he was released. However, New York filed a civil lawsuit against Tweed in an attempt to recover some of the stolen money. He fled to Spain, where he was recognized because of Nast's cartoon images of him. Tweed was recaptured and sent to jail. He died in prison in 1878.

Tammany Hall and its leaders continued to influence and control New York City politics for decades afterward.

Chapter 7 – Societal and Skyline Restructurings

After the downfall of Tweed, Tammany Hall gained a more reputable leader in "Honest" John Kelly. He was credited with removing many of Tweed's inner circle. As a savvier leader and politician, Kelly was able to revitalize Tammany Hall's influence. The group successfully supported and was able to elect many Democrats in city and state elections.

As more and more immigrants arrived in the city, they were welcomed to their new lives by Tammany Hall ward leaders. Tammany Hall and its members were there to help find housing, food, and jobs for those who supported them. This continued to infuse more power into the Tammany Hall leadership.

Though the political machine of Tammany Hall continued almost unabated after the arrest of Tweed, that opening in its armor was enough to let in other reformers who built upon the work of Thomas Nast. These reformers worked to improve the conditions of those living in tenement housing in New York City.

Tenements or tenant houses were erected in the early 1800s for the burgeoning population of immigrants. City regulations required building lots that were twenty-five feet wide and one hundred feet long for tenements. Most buildings encompassed the entire piece of land. Tenements often had only one foot of space between each building. Therefore, the dwellings had little to no circulation or natural light. Only apartments that faced the street had a window.

These units also lacked indoor plumbing; shared bathroom facilities were located outside. Most tenements did not have lighting in the hallways, so nightly trips to the outdoor toilet were accomplished in the dark. Though many streets had gas, sewer, and water lines, tenements were not connected to any of these utilities.

Most tenements had four to six floors, with each floor divided into four apartments. Often, the apartments were less than 350 square feet and were home to families of up to ten people. Units had two or three rooms at the most. Parlors were used for additional sleeping space at night to complement the one bedroom in the tenement.

By the turn of the century, it is estimated that two-thirds of all New York City dwellers lived in overcrowded tenements. Just under 2.4 million people inhabited the more than 80,000 tenement buildings that had been constructed.

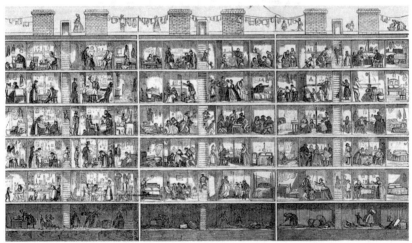

Illustration of a side view of 38 Cherry Street, New York.

The severe overcrowding of the spaces and the unsanitary conditions caused the rapid spread of germs and disease. In 1849, a cholera epidemic swept through the city and killed more than five thousand people. Other epidemics of typhus, tuberculosis, and diphtheria caused continual struggles for tenement dwellers.

Calls for change and improved living conditions were led by city doctors in 1864. Due to their concerns about the lack of sanitation in New York City, the Council of Hygiene and Public Health was formed.

The council assessed the conditions in the city, particularly the tenements.

As a result of the council's report and the efforts of city physicians, the First Tenement Act of 1867 was passed into law. This act defined tenements as rentals that housed more than three separate families. The law developed regulations for construction. Some of the requirements included the need for one privy or toilet per twenty people, fire escapes, and ventilators or windows in each room where people slept.

For most tenants, their housing situation did not change after the law was passed. Ensuring that the stipulations in the law were enacted did not routinely occur. However, the law did set the stage for follow-up legislation. In 1879, an amendment to the First Tenement Act was passed into law.

One provision of the newer law included the need for more windows. These were referred to as tuberculosis windows since they were intended to increase and improve air quality and flow within the apartments. Better ventilation would help fight the diseases that devastated the people living in the tenements.

However, the landlords were reluctant to spend money. Many building owners installed interior windows instead to save money. These did not address the problem of circulating air and improving living conditions.

Little changed with the passage of either piece of legislation. Tenements remained horribly overcrowded and a breeding ground for disease. It was not until *How the Other Half Lives* was published in 1890 that significant changes slowly began to happen.

Jacob Riis was a photographer, journalist, and author of the photo essay that exposed the horrors of tenements in New York City. While other articles had been published detailing life as an immigrant living in a tenement, Riis's background and approach made an incredible and long-lasting impact on the upper class's view of poverty.

Riis, who was an immigrant himself, lived in poverty when he first arrived in the United States. He fully understood the struggle. Years of hard work eventually landed Riis a job as a newspaper reporter. In the role of crime reporter for the *New-York Tribune*, Riis was frequently in downtrodden neighborhoods with the police. During these ventures, Riis saw the terrible living situations of many city residents.

One of the elements that made Riis's exposé impactful was his use of a camera. Pictures brought his words to life. Images of garbage-strewn streets and alleyways patrolled by local gangs, malnourished children dressed in worn and dirty clothing, and gaunt adults packed into tiny, overcrowded spaces began to sway the opinion of other New Yorkers and spur them into action.

One of Riis's photos. This one depicts sleeping homeless children.
https://commons.wikimedia.org/wiki/File:Sleeping,_homeless_children_-_Jacob_Riis.jpg

From one immigrant neighborhood to the next, Riis humanized the people trapped in their repulsive tenements. Captions added depth to the situations. Riis noted how twelve adults would be crammed into a thirteen-foot room to sleep and how there was an infant mortality rate of one in ten babies.

One of the outcomes of the publication of *How the Other Half Lives* and the work of other reformers was the creation of the Tenement House Committee, or THC, in 1894. Also referred to as the Gilder Committee after its chairperson, Richard Gilder, the THC performed a thorough exploration of tenement housing. Riis, though not officially a member of the committee, consulted with them.

The THC crafted legislation to improve the living conditions of the majority of New York City residents. The demolition of Five Points, which was beyond repair, was recommended and enacted. The Tenement House Law of 1901 required indoor plumbing, larger lot sizes, access to natural light and air, fire escapes, and more. Riis and his camera made an indelible impact on many lives.

A woman who influenced Riis, Nellie Bly, a pseudonym for Elizabeth Cochran Seaman, also sought to reform and improve the lives of New Yorkers. When Bly first moved to the city and was seeking employment, she pitched a story about the immigrant experience to the *New York World*. Instead of that story, Joseph Pulitzer, the editor of the paper, wanted an investigative article about the conditions on New York City's Blackwell's Island.

Pulitzer's managing editor, Colonel John Cockerill, provided Bly with the details of the task. Bly was charged with investigating allegations of patient abuse at the mental health asylum. Cockerill assigned Bly the name Nellie Brown to use for her mission.

First, Bly obtained a room at a women's boarding house. After taking a room at the Temporary Home for Females, No. 84 Second Avenue, Bly continually asked others for details about her travel trunks. She wanted other residents and the matrons to see her as a poor, newly arrived immigrant. Her shabby physical appearance and seemingly incoherent mental capacity soon bothered the other boarders. The matron of the boarding house summoned the police.

At the Essex Market Police Courtroom, Judge Patrick Duffy assumed that Bly was a Cuban immigrant, a presumption that Bly did not correct. Bias against newly arrived immigrants included the belief that they were more apt to have mental health issues. Bly was ordered to the insane ward at Bellevue Hospital. There, she was examined by four different doctors; each proclaimed her mentally incompetent.

Bly was ferried to Blackwell's Island Women's Lunatic Asylum on a boat filled with grubby and confused women. For most, the trip to Blackwell's Island, now Roosevelt Island, was one way; patients did not leave.

Bly documented her own experiences and what she witnessed happen to others. Her notes talked about how patients were subjected to beatings, fed putrefied food, and bathed in unsanitary and cold water. Verbal abuse and neglect added to the horrific conditions and treatment of the women.

The ratio of one doctor to one hundred patients made patient care almost impossible. Bly noted that only two doctors attempted to treat the women. Patients were often isolated in rat-infested rooms and/or made to sit for hours on benches and not permitted to talk or read.

Bly reported that many women, including herself, did not display indications of mental illness. Women whom Bly interviewed were sent to Blackwell's Island because of language barriers, collapsing from physical work and poverty or even by malicious husbands.

A lawyer from the *New York World* had to be sent to rescue Bly from the asylum. Her first section of "Behind Asylum Bars" was published on October 9th, 1887. The first installment was so well received that newspapers from all over the country printed Bly's piece. Her entire experience was assembled, and the exposé was published as a book, *Ten Days in a Mad-House*, with Bly's illustrations.

Twenty-three-year-old Nellie Bly was one of the first investigative journalists. Her undercover work led to changes in how New York City diagnosed and treated those with mental health ailments. The city convened a grand jury to investigate Blackwell's Island. Better food, cleaner facilities, and translators were some of the changes that were implemented to improve the conditions of the female patients. Doctors and other staff who abused the patients were fired.

Contrasting the living conditions of many New Yorkers was the emerging skyline of the city. One of the first massive undertakings that changed the vista of New York City was the Brooklyn Bridge.

A supporter of the bridge was Boss Tweed. Allegedly, unless Tweed and his Tammany Hall cronies approved of a venture, the project would not happen. At his trial for corruption, Tweed reported that he organized bribes of up to $65,000 to send to city leaders to ensure their votes of approval. As a member of the bridge committee that oversaw finances, Tweed had hoped to skim his share of the money. However, his 1871 arrest prevented him from fulfilling that plan.

Even with Tweed in jail, the project to design and build the Brooklyn Bridge continued. The bridge was larger and longer than any bridge built before it, and it altered the skyline of New York City. With its verticality, the bridge's towers were seven times taller than many of the city's current four-story structures.

John Roebling, the chief engineer on the project, began designing the bridge as early as 1857. However, the Civil War paused Roebling's dream to span the East River. Roebling was considered the lead bridge designer at the time. His schematics included using wire ropes fabricated from steel that he designed. This was the first bridge that would be made of steel instead of cable wire.

Construction on the bridge commenced in 1869. That summer, Roebling's toes were crushed in an accident while he was taking compass readings. A few weeks later, Roebling succumbed to tetanus. His son, Washington Roebling, assumed his father's leadership role. To check on the progress of the project, Washington journeyed into the water in a caisson (a large watertight chamber). Compressed air was pumped into the airtight structures that transported workers through the water so they could perform underwater tasks. Washington contracted decompression sickness or the bends as a result of his time in the caisson. Washington Roebling was paralyzed as a result.

Washington Roebling managed the project from his apartment. Using field glass to monitor progress, Roebling sent directives to the workers through his wife, Emily. Not a professionally trained engineer, Emily was self-taught. For the last ten years of the building project, Emily was the lead on-site engineer. Since she was a woman, Emily did not receive recognition for her work.

During the fourteen years of construction, at least one hundred workers were afflicted by the bends or decompression illness. Estimates suggest that at least twenty-five workers died as a result of construction accidents.

On May 24th, 1883, the almost 1600-foot Brooklyn Bridge opened; it was the longest suspension bridge in the world. President Chester Arthur was on hand to lead the celebration. Emily Roebling was the first person to cross the bridge in an open-air carriage.

Newspaper announcing the opening of the Brooklyn Bridge.

The Brooklyn Bridge was an engineering marvel of steel and electricity, and its towers began to define the New York City skyline. At 278 feet, the towers were the tallest human-made structure in the

Western Hemisphere. Another legacy of the Brooklyn Bridge was the connection between Brooklyn and Manhattan. This paved the way for the creation of Greater New York with its five boroughs.

There had been discussions about consolidating the five boroughs into one city for decades. Those who supported the movement visualized a stronger and more influential New York City. Combining each borough's cultural and commercial assets could position the city to be viewed and treated as the leading city of the nation and the world. There would also be a sharing of resources that would make the boroughs more efficient.

However, not everyone in the boroughs was in favor of this vision. Some of their greatest concerns were the politics of Manhattan and the influence of Tammany Hall. The corruption of Tammany Hall and the money that was paid in bribes was problematic for Brooklyn residents. They also feared the power and control that Tammany Hall held over elected officials in Manhattan. Brooklynites wanted to retain their independence.

The decision was put to the public in a referendum in 1884, one year after the completion of the Brooklyn Bridge. By a 277, or 50.1 percent margin, 64,744 citizens voted for the creation of Greater New York. At that time, New York City was the largest city in America and the second-largest in the world. Manhattan was selected to be the location for the city's government.

The year 1884 was also when skyscrapers became infused in the vocabulary and use of architectural design. Chicago is credited with building the first skyscraper in 1885 with its Home Life Insurance Building. New York City was not going to be outdone. Once the Department of Buildings approved steel skeleton-frame construction in 1892, the steel-framed Tower Building was built in 1889. Designed by architect Bradford Lee Gilbert, the interior steel structure of the Tower Building provided its support, not the masonry on the outside of the building.

Technological developments and engineering advances made the fabrication of taller buildings possible. Steel was a key component in providing the framework for these buildings, similar to how steel and wire rope proved essential to the construction of the Brooklyn Bridge. Brick buildings were limited in their height due to the weight of their walls. Otis's success with his elevators as part of the Exhibition of the

Works of Industry of All Nations held in New York City in 1853 was another component of the success of skyscrapers.

Lower Manhattan's bedrock provided a solid foothold for the ever-growing number and size of skyscrapers. With the city population continuing to expand, going from over 1.2 million in 1880 to 3.4 million at the turn of the century, upward construction was needed to accommodate residents and businesses.

The iconic Flatiron Building was constructed in 1902. Its architect, Daniel Burnham, designed the building to maximize the piece of land. Because its shape resembles a flatiron, that became the building's name instead of the George A. Fuller Company. At the intersection of Broadway and Fifth Avenue, the building provided some of the best vistas of the city.

Construction of the Flatiron Building.

Cass Gilbert designed the Woolworth Building, which was constructed in 1913. From the time of the building's opening until 1930, the Woolworth Building held the distinction of being the world's tallest building. With the moniker the "Cathedral of Commerce," the Gothic 54-story and 792-foot-tall tower was considered one of the most beautiful buildings in the city.

It was also one of the most technologically advanced structures. The Woolworth Building had the fastest elevator at the time, steam-powered heat, and electricity. Frank W. Woolworth, the owner of a massive chain of five-and-dime stores across the country, paid for his thirteen-million-dollar skyscraper in cash.

The construction of skyscrapers throughout the city was unregulated until New York passed its 1916 Zoning Resolution. Land in the city would now be zoned by use. There were three main categories detailed in the resolution: residential, commercial, and unrestricted, which was usually industrial. To ensure that streets had air flow and natural light, the resolution controlled the shapes of tall buildings. Therefore, as buildings grew taller, they needed to become skinnier. This created the "wedding cake" tiered style of construction.

Chapter 8 – The Big Apple

New York City continued to grow in prominence as a significant city in the country and the world. In the 1920s, the moniker of the Big Apple was associated with the city. In *The Morning Telegraph*, John J. Fitz Gerald, its sports writer, authored an article about racecourses and horse races that were located in the metropolitan area.

Fitz Gerald had overheard African American stable workers in New Orleans refer to New York City as the "big apple." The reference was because the city's racetracks were considered to be the big league in racing. Bettors used the term "big red apple" when making wagers.

The name expanded beyond the world of sports. It took hold in the music world as well. Musicians who played in New York City venues referred to those as the "big apple" or a "big-time appearance."

In 1925, New York City passed London in size and became the largest metropolitan area in the world. Immigrants continued to arrive in the city through Ellis Island. The city's skyline, with its well-known skyscrapers, flourished. Grand Central Terminal and Pennsylvania Station facilitated passengers arriving to and departing from the city by train.

For many New Yorkers, the 1920s was a decade of unabashed opulence. The Roaring Twenties brought a newness to cities, which many sought after enduring the horrors of World War I. An optimistic spirit infused many as the city and the country entered an era of modernity. A different world began unfolding with automobiles, new styles of music, motion pictures, evolving roles for women, and changing social demographics.

New York became a destination for many African Americans who sought a better life. From 1917 to 1925, more than 200,000 African Americans moved from the South to New York City. The Great Migration started in part because of the labor shortages in the North. Fewer people were emigrating from European countries because of World War I. Once the United States became embroiled in the war, American men were sent overseas, so they were no longer part of the workforce. African Americans were recruited by companies to fill the labor void.

For many African Americans who joined the Great Migration, they had hopes of improving their economic situations by obtaining non-agricultural jobs. Southern agricultural opportunities as sharecroppers did not provide a lucrative financial situation. Also, many Southern farms had been decimated by the boll weevil.

Not only did the North offer the hope for better jobs, but it also did not have explicit Jim Crow laws. Many Southern states passed Jim Crow laws after the Civil War. These laws permitted and enforced racial segregation.

The population of African Americans in the North increased by almost 20 percent. Growth in the cities was much higher, with New York experiencing an over 65 percent increase in its Black population. Many who participated in the Great Migration to New York City settled in Harlem.

Many neighborhoods in the North were not welcoming or receptive to Black Americans. Northern communities, including New York City, experienced the phenomenon of White flight. When African Americans moved into the area, White residents left. In Harlem, over eighty-seven thousand Black people arrived in the 1920s. During the same decade, almost 120,000 Whites moved from Harlem. By the end of the decade, Harlem's population of Blacks was more than 70 percent.

Philip Payton Jr. paved the way for Harlem's new residents from the Great Migration. In the late 1800s, Harlem had been designed to become an enclave for wealthy White New Yorkers. However, overbuilding created an excess of available housing, which caused a real estate crash.

Picture of Philip Payton Jr.

Other sections of New York were no longer available or welcoming to Blacks. Race riots that stemmed from the 1900 killing of a policeman by an African American created inhospitable neighborhoods. Also, to enable the formation of Penn Station, neighborhoods were eliminated.

Payton saw this as an opportunity to help African Americans find housing in Harlem. His company, the Afro-American Realty Company, was formed in 1904 with funding from other Black investors. Payton sought to make a financial profit for himself and his investors, along with trying to address the issues of housing and race.

Afro-American Realty sold three tenements to the Hudson Realty Company in 1905. Hudson purchased the properties because they abutted land it wanted to sell to investors for development. The land would have more value if it bordered buildings with White occupants, so Hudson Realty evicted the Black renters.

Not to be outdone, Payton's company then purchased two adjacent tenements. They evicted the White residents and rented the properties to Black people. Hudson's properties sat unrented, which caused the company to lose money. Hudson eventually conceded and resold the first three buildings back to Payton and his company. Hudson Realty suffered significant losses.

Payton's work in Harlem paved the way for many of those involved in the mass movement of African Americans in the 1920s. Considered the "Father of Harlem," his real estate company and its ventures helped precipitate the cultural era known as the Harlem Renaissance.

The Red Summer of 1919 is considered to be another event that contributed to the Harlem Renaissance. The term "Red Summer" is attributed to the NAACP (National Association for the Advancement of Colored People) secretary at the time, James Weldon Johnson. Race riots, lynchings, and violence toward Black people that occurred during the summer of 1919 were explored in the pieces created by Harlem artists.

Some of the tension that led to the riots and violence of the Red Summer can be attributed to the return of soldiers who fought in World War I. One unit from New York City, the 369th Infantry Regiment, was an all-Black unit due to racial segregation. During their training at Camp Whitman, the unit suffered racial insults and attacks from the White soldiers who were with other units. Most all-Black troops were not sent to fight on the front lines because they were viewed as inferior soldiers and ineffective combatants.

Soldiers of the 369th Infantry Regiment.
https://commons.wikimedia.org/wiki/File:369th_15th_New_York.jpg

However, when the 369th arrived in France in March 1918, General John Pershing, who was the commander of the American Expeditionary Forces, assigned them to the struggling French forces. French military leaders sent the 369th to fight in the Champagne Region's Argonne Forest.

The unit, whose members called themselves the Harlem's Rattlers, fought valiantly beside their French counterparts for 191 straight days of combat, longer than any other unit from America. Their fighting prowess against the Germans in the Meuse-Argonne Offensive earned the 369th Infantry Regiment the moniker Hollenkampfer, or "hellfighter." They were then known as the Harlem Hellfighters, and the unit earned the prestigious service award of the Croix de Guerre from the French government.

The Harlem Hellfighters received vastly different treatment upon their return to US soil. Though Black Americans fought with honor and courage during World War I, their reentry into society was often met with open and violent hostility. Competition for jobs added to the brewing resentment toward Blacks.

In July of the Red Summer, there was an altercation between a White man and a Black man. They got into an angry discussion about the war. One of the men began randomly shooting and struck two people with his bullets. This caused word to spread that there was a riot brewing between 2nd and 3rd Avenue. Crowds formed, and more shots were fired.

Claude McKay, one of the Harlem Renaissance writers, captured the violence and fears of the Red Summer in "If We Must Die." His poem addresses Black Americans defending their rights and lives during a summer that saw numerous lynchings of Blacks. McKay's poem is considered a pivotal foundation of literature since he speaks directly to Blacks and encourages each person to defend themselves. The speaker of the poem joins in the resistance against oppressors and creates a timeless call to challenge and overcome inequities in all societies.

McKay was one of the many talented artists who helped create a new sense of one's abilities and rights within the Black community. Sharing details of Black struggles, inequities, and culture was part of the Harlem Renaissance. It was time for Black creators and authors to control the message of what Blackness was and was not. No issue was too sensitive to capture. Issues of race, racism, economics, social class, gender, and more were expressed through music, dance, poetry, literature, and art.

The music of the Harlem Renaissance featured many jazz and blues performers. The Cotton Club was a key venue for many Black musicians, who played in front of all-White audiences. Some of the well-known African American entertainers associated with the Cotton Club and the music of Harlem include the house bands of Fletcher Henderson, Duke Ellington, Cab Calloway, and Jimmie Lunceford. Louis Armstrong and his trumpet and distinctive voice graced the clubs of Harlem. Bessie Smith, Billie Holliday, and Ella Fitzgerald also transformed the blues and jazz.

Picture of the Cotton Club.
https://commons.wikimedia.org/wiki/File:Cotton_Club_1930.jpg

The first Black woman to perform in a motion picture with sound was Josephine Baker. Her debut in *The Jazz Singer* made her a movie star. Many other singers, dancers, and musicians transformed music with their performances during the Harlem Renaissance.

Music was forever altered, as was the world of visual arts. Artists, such as Aaron Douglas, captured images of everyday life in Harlem, along with depictions of the collective and individual experiences of African Americans.

Authors of the Harlem Renaissance shared their ideas and talents through a broad array of genres. Langston Hughes and Louis Armstrong influenced each other's works, weaving jazz and poetry together. Other writers, including Zora Neale Hurston, Jean Toomer, and Countee Cullen, portrayed issues of racism in American society. They worked to erase negative stereotypes that White people had of Blacks.

The Harlem Renaissance left a lasting impact on the arts in America.

Harlem and the other sections of New York City experienced the restrictions of the Volstead Act, also known as Prohibition. In 1920, the sale and manufacture of alcohol was illegal in the country; this law would be in effect for the next thirteen years. However, the consumption of alcohol continued almost unabated.

In New York City, it is believed thirty-two thousand speakeasy clubs operated throughout Prohibition. These clubs were called speakeasies because they required patrons to speak the secret access code to enter the club. Speakeasies were illegal during Prohibition, but with so many establishments hidden in basements, backrooms, and even in plain sight, it was impossible for law enforcement to raid every saloon.

With each legal bar that was forced to close after the law went into effect, it is estimated that six illegal speakeasy clubs opened in its place. With so many clubs operating in the city, there was competition for customers. Jazz and blues bands performed in the "gin" joints, not just in Harlem but throughout all five boroughs.

Alcohol sold in the speakeasies was sold to them by bootleggers or made in home stills. The poorer quality alcohol was mixed with ginger ale, colas, or juices, which created cocktails. The demand for alcohol created a vast illegal enterprise. "Bootleg" became a common term during Prohibition; it refers to a person hiding alcohol bottles in their tall boots.

New York City experienced the emergence of an organized crime network in the 1920s. Previously, gangs tended to operate in their ethnic neighborhoods. However, many postulate that New York City became the epicenter of organized crime as a result of Prohibition. With its harbor, New York City was a perfect location to smuggle alcohol to, which earned it the title of one of the alcohol capitals of the country.

Salvatore Luciano was in one of the neighborhood gangs of Five Points. The young Luciano made career connections with other local gang members; for instance, he made connections with Meyer Lansky and Benjamin Siegel (known as Bugsy) from the Jewish gang.

Mug shot of Luciano.
https://commons.wikimedia.org/wiki/File:Lucky_Luciano_mugshot_1931.jpg

Later, Luciano joined Giuseppe Masseria's enterprise. For "Joe the Boss" (Masseria), Luciano dealt drugs and pimped women. In 1916, Luciano was sent to reform school for dealing heroin. The advent of Prohibition created the opportunity to supply alcohol to Manhattan's new underground bars. By the middle of the decade, Luciano's operation was the largest in the city, which caused him to rise in status and power within Masseria's organization.

Lucky Luciano, as he was later known, was part of the younger generation called the Young Turks. He wanted to expand the Italian organizations. The Young Turks wanted to include gangs of other ethnicities. Eventually, Luciano was able to establish the Commission in 1931. The intent was to share the power between five families and eliminate the rule of the Sicilians. Luciano is seen as the father of the modern American Mafia.

The end of the 1920s not only saw a change in the leadership of organized crime families but also marked the end of the era of opulence. Many factors created the Roaring Twenties. After the brutality that soldiers experienced during World War I, people sought a respite from the horrors of war. Additionally, new and exciting consumer products were available, and they could all be bought on credit. Speakeasies welcomed women, who were finding new freedoms, including the right to vote.

Wall Street and the New York Stock Exchange joined in the euphoria. The Dow Jones Industrial Average grew from a low of 63 to 381 by September 1929, which was a six-fold increase. On October 28th, 1929, known as Black Monday, the market lost almost 13 percent of its value. The next day, Black Tuesday, the Dow dropped almost 12 percent more. The valuation of the market continued to decline for the next three years to an all-time low of forty-one. This translates into an 89 percent decline. It was not until November 1954, twenty-five years, that the market would return to its pre-crash levels.

The panic that resulted from the market crash caused a run on the banks. People could no longer afford to pay back the money they had borrowed. Banks lost millions of dollars. Unemployment soared. The Great Depression had begun, ending the expansion of skyscrapers that were defining the New York City skyline.

However, two major construction projects defined New York's response to the Great Depression. The first was the creation of Rockefeller Center; the other project was the construction of the Empire State Building.

Rockefeller Center was the vision of John D. Rockefeller Jr., who sought to create a "city within a city." Sitting on twenty-two acres, the fourteen original commercial buildings are located between 48th and 51st Street.

Originally, the plan had been to construct a new home for the Metropolitan Opera, along with other commercial buildings. After the crash of the stock market, the opera company withdrew from the agreement. Now, Rockefeller held the lease to the land on his own. He also lost half of his family's fortune in the crash.

Lunch atop a Skyscraper.
https://en.wikipedia.org/wiki/File:Lunch_atop_a_Skyscraper_-_Charles_Clyde_Ebbets.jpg

Nevertheless, Rockefeller decided to pursue the project. Speakeasies, shops, and boarding houses occupied the land at the beginning of the project. Throughout the eleven years of construction, Rockefeller was able to employ between forty thousand and sixty thousand workers.

Rockefeller Center was the first complex of its kind. Included in the development were retail stores, office spaces, restaurants, broadcasting studios, and Radio City Music Hall. After Rockefeller learned about systems that could make artificial ice, a skating rink was added to the design and built in 1936. Other features included air conditioning and high-speed elevators.

In 1931, the first Christmas tree was decorated at Rockefeller Center. Workers put their money together so they could afford a twenty-foot balsam fir tree. Decorations were all homemade by the workers' families. The annual tradition for the lighting of the Christmas tree began in 1933 with a fifty-foot tree.

Another inspirational building was constructed as part of a contest to be the world's tallest building. Even the onset of the Great Depression was not going to stop the design and formation of the Empire State Building. For forty years, it held the title of the world's tallest building.

Construction took place on the site of the former Waldorf-Astoria between 34th and 33rd Street at Fifth Avenue. Pieces of the hotel were auctioned, which earned money for the project. The construction firm was selected in October 1929, the same month as the stock market crash. The financier of the project, John Jacob Raskob, had been born in poverty and, with hard work, became financially successful. Even when facing the Great Depression, he remained optimistic in the American system.

William Lamb designed the structure in just two weeks. Construction commenced on March 17th, 1930, and was completed in one year and forty-five days. Over 3,400 workers helped in the building; they completed two and a half floors each week.

Photograph of a workman on the framework of the Empire State Building.
https://en.wikipedia.org/wiki/File:Old_timer_structural_worker2.jpg

Two hundred and ten steel columns comprise the vertical frame of the building. More than sixty tons of steel were used in the construction of the frame. More than ten million bricks were used, along with 200,000 cubic feet of limestone. The Empire State Building is 102 stories and stands 1,250 feet tall, but with its antenna, the building soars to 1,454 feet.

New York was ready to enter a new era. In 1933, New Yorkers elected a new mayor, Fiorello La Guardia. He was up to the task of continuing the successes of the Empire State Building and Rockefeller Center. La Guardia held the mayor's office for three consecutive terms. He governed without the influence of Tammany Hall. La Guardia addressed corruption in the city and helped lead New York out of the Great Depression.

Chapter 9 – Many Sides of the Big Apple

October 29th, 1929, drastically altered the lives of New Yorkers. Record levels of unemployment and underemployment created financial struggles and challenges for years. In New York City, almost one-third of all residents lost their jobs. The underemployed were compelled to accept dramatic reductions in their income to retain or find jobs.

Hoovervilles, or an area in which homeless people lived, sprang up throughout the city, including on the lawns of Central Park. To feed themselves and their families, people lined up in long bread lines to obtain day-old (and older) leftovers from bakeries. Soup kitchens throughout the city sustained many.

Projects, such as the construction of Rockefeller Center and the Empire State Building, were not large enough to pull New York City from the depths of the Great Depression. When La Guardia became mayor in 1934, it was a boost to the city and to the president of the country. The relationship between Franklin D. Roosevelt (FDR) and La Guardia helped cement many of the programs that FDR included as part of his New Deal. New York City and its mayor were sounding boards for FDR's ideas to lead the country out of the Great Depression.

In return, New York received more federal funding than any other location in the country. More than 700,000 New Yorkers were employed in jobs created by the New Deal. Under the Works Progress Administration (WPA) and La Guardia's leadership, New York City was transformed. More than one thousand projects, from art murals to funding for and building of schools, hospitals, parks, transportation infrastructure, and housing, were funded as part of the WPA in New York City.

Some of the work completed in the city as part of FDR's New Deal included New York City's first commercial airport. When it opened in 1939, it was called the New York Municipal Airport; it was renamed La Guardia Airport in 1947. Another WPA project connected Midtown Manhattan and Weehawken, New Jersey; the Lincoln Tunnel opened for traffic in December 1937.

Poster from the WPA.
https://commons.wikimedia.org/wiki/File:Ny-airports-wpa-poster.jpg

Other transformative projects completed in the city with federal funding from the New Deal were the restoration of Bryant Park, the East River (later FDR) Drive, the Triborough Bridge, and the Henry Hudson Parkway. Additionally, swimming pools, parks, and playgrounds were constructed throughout the five boroughs.

While these projects forever changed the city's landscape, they did not fully restore New York City's economy. However, the country's industrial and commercial requirements to enter World War II facilitated the full economic recovery of the city.

At the commencement of the war, New York already claimed the title of the world's largest city with its more than seven million inhabitants, and the Empire State Building was the tallest skyscraper in the world. Economically, the city's harbor processed 40 percent of the country's shipping freight. New York was an industrial powerhouse, producing a wider range of items and more volume than any other city in the world. Wall Street and its affiliated businesses made the city the financial center of the world, and more than 130 of the country's top 500 industrial corporations filled the city's skyscrapers and other buildings.

War-related businesses and production in New York City contributed to the success of the Allied forces and continued to help grow the city. Over 700,000 war-related manufacturing jobs were created, with people working in hundreds of new factories and industries. New Yorkers' broad scope of products included military uniforms, penicillin, tents, plane parts, and much more.

More than seventy-five thousand Brooklyn Navy Yard employees worked around the clock. Encompassing 290 acres, the Navy Yard produced more ships than Japan during the war. Ships constructed in other shipyards were fitted with their armaments in Brooklyn. Warships needing repairs also found their way to the Brooklyn Navy Yard.

Picture of Brooklyn Navy Yard, 1945.
https://commons.wikimedia.org/wiki/File:New_York_Navy_Yard_aerial_photo_1_in_April_194
5.jpg

New York's role in supporting the United States and Allied troops contributed to many successful military campaigns and the eventual victory of the Allied forces. An enduring legacy of World War II originated in the research facilities at Columbia University and offices on Broadway. In 1939, Enrico Fermi, Walter Zinn, Leo Szilard, and Herbert Anderson tested and experimented with nuclear fission. Located in the basement of Pupin Physics Laboratories, the scientists split the uranium atom to form the basis for the atomic bomb using nuclear fission.

In the summer of 1942, the army assumed control of the next steps to develop the atomic bomb. Colonel James Marshall received orders to establish the Laboratory for the Development of Substitute Metals, or DSM, in New York for the Army Corps of Engineers. Marshall set up offices on the eighteenth floor of 270 Broadway and established the Manhattan Engineer District, which followed the army's protocol of naming engineering commands after the city in which they were established. A top-secret mission during the war, the atomic bomb project became known as the Manhattan Project.

As the project grew in scope, it needed to be relocated to a less populated area. The Broadway offices were closed, but the development of the Manhattan Project continued. A new age of atomic weaponry was ushered in.

When troops returned home after the end of World War II, they were greeted with a new age of prosperity and consumerism. Americans, weary from the war and the Great Depression, sought to capitalize on the newness that the 1950s offered. Factories shifted from wartime production to supplying a plethora of modern goods. Wages increased, and credit was more readily available. People were encouraged to purchase televisions, washing machines, and more.

Two purchases that dramatically affected the landscape of New York City were automobiles and homeownership.

Veterans returning from war found it difficult to locate housing in New York City. The lack of new construction during the Great Depression and the war caused a housing shortage. That, coupled with a G.I. Bill that provided veterans with funding for college and purchasing homes, created new opportunities for many. Veterans were able to return to school and obtain better-paying jobs. Additionally, returning war veterans could purchase homes with no money down.

New York City's lack of available housing prompted the creation of a massive development just twenty miles from Manhattan. Before serving in the Navy in World War II, William Levitt had obtained the right to build on four thousand acres of potato fields. This flat farmland was the perfect place for Levitt to construct subdivisions and create suburbia.

Levitt developed a method to mass-produce homes, similar to the mass production employed by automotive factories. Houses were constructed in twenty-seven steps. None of the homes had basements, which made construction faster. Within four years, over seventeen thousand homes were constructed just miles from New York City. More than eighty-two thousand people moved to the suburbs, many having migrated from the city. This began what is frequently termed the White flight from the city.

Two aspects that made life in the suburbs appealing to veterans were the desire to escape from the horrors of the war and begin anew and the open highways. After the war, automobile companies restarted their mass production of cars. Additionally, the federal government passed the Interstate Highway Act. This provided significant funding to pay for the maze of roads within the city, connecting New York City to the new suburbs.

Leading and controlling New York City's direction in housing, transportation, and parks during the transition into the modern era (and for decades before it) was Robert Moses. From 1924 until 1968, Robert Moses was involved in or headed public agencies that dealt with public works in New York City. His impact on planning the city included projects during the Roaring Twenties, the Great Depression, World War II, and the modern era after the war.

Picture of Robert Moses.
https://commons.wikimedia.org/wiki/File:Robert_Moses_with_Battery_Bridge_model.jpg

Throughout his tenure, Moses is credited with building parks, playgrounds, beaches, pools, zoos, parkways, highways, tunnels, bridges, and housing. It is believed that, all told, Moses's projects cost more than twenty-seven billion dollars. More than 500,000 people were displaced due to the projects. New replaced old, which meant small neighborhoods often gave way to massive highways.

To address the housing shortage after World War II, the federal government passed the 1949 Housing Act. When Moses was made aware of this act, he formed the Committee on Slum Clearance. His political, financial, and real estate connections were placed on the committee. Moses named himself chairperson of the committee.

One component of the act provided funding to New York City to purchase blighted land and/or slums under eminent domain. Cities were expected to work with developers and create new livable spaces for their residents. A stipulation of the act was that all buildings in the designated section needed to be demolished, which resulted in the destruction of entire communities and neighborhoods. Ways of life were eliminated.

Intended but not mandated as part of the federal 1949 Housing Act was the rebuilding of housing that displaced residents could afford. However, New York City's use of eminent domain resulted in the eviction of hundreds of thousands of residents. The new housing or structures built in their former neighborhoods were created for people with more income.

Any new housing built as part of the plan was large, modern, massive structures. They lacked easy access to the streets since they did not have front stoops or windows near the sidewalks. Neighborhood stores and restaurants were not rebuilt as part of the program.

Under the program, Moses constructed the Lincoln Center. To add this cultural building, he had the San Juan Hill neighborhood demolished. This step forced the relocation of over seven thousand families. Not only were families displaced under the guise of slum clearance, but eight hundred businesses were also shuttered or forced to move to create the Lincoln Center for the Creative and Performing Arts.

Though city officials promised to assist displaced residents, alternate housing was not available. Demolition outpaced new construction. Only about 20 percent of those who were relocated during slum removals were able to find comparable housing.

Another aspect of urban planning that occurred after the war and into the 1950s was the construction of highways to meet the demands of commuters to and from the city. To construct highways, Moses agreed to build through existing neighborhoods. More than 1,500 families lost their homes and were displaced to clear land for the Cross Bronx Expressway. Residents were informed of the demise of their neighborhoods in a letter sent on December 4th, 1952. They had only ninety days to pack up and move so that progress could occur.

Aerial picture of the demolition site.
John Rooney, CC BY-SA 4.0 <https://creativecommons.org/licenses/by-sa/4.0>, via Wikimedia Commons; https://commons.wikimedia.org/wiki/File:San-juan-hill-demolition-1962.jpg

New York was not only losing traditional neighborhoods; at least two other iconic structures were viewed as obsolete as society's needs evolved. In 1954, the immigration and detention centers at Ellis Island were closed when the Immigration and Naturalization Service removed Norwegian seaman Arne Peterssen from the island for overstaying his time in the US. Peterssen was returned to his home country.

The first immigrant welcomed through the "Gateway to America" was Annie Moore from Ireland in 1892. In the intervening years, more than twelve million immigrants were processed through Ellis Island. Named after Samuel Ellis, who bought the land in 1774, the island served many purposes. Ellis built a tavern on the land, which, at that point, was a little more than three acres.

Landfill was added to increase the size of the island to five acres in 1905. The additional land was used to create a contagious disease ward.

During World War I, when there was a dramatic decline in immigrants, the island supported the navies of the Allied forces as a waystation. Ships were able to resupply at the island. Ellis Island's hospital supplied beds for wounded servicemen. Enemies were also detained on the island.

In the 1930s, concern about conditions on the island prompted the creation of the Ellis Island Committee. They recommended the addition of more buildings and facilities to process immigrants. More landfill was brought to the island, and it grew to 27.5 acres.

After US consulates were able to process immigrants, Ellis Island's role shifted to a detention and deportation facility that housed and processed illegal immigrants. During World War II, the government's enemies and supporters of the Nazi regime were detained on the island. As with WWI, the hospital facilities were used for the military.

After the war, the number of detainees housed on Ellis Island shrank dramatically. By 1953, there were just under 250 captives. Since there were also about 250 staff members to house the detainees, Ellis Island was soon classified as surplus government property in 1955.

Responsibility for the island was transferred to the National Park Service in 1965. The buildings and the island fell into a state of disrepair. Cleanup efforts were initiated. In 1984, $156 million was allocated to renovate Ellis Island.

Entrance to the main building on Ellis Island.

Another New York landmark was demolished before it could be saved from destruction. Penn Station fell victim to reduced ridership due to the increase in automobiles and highways in the city. Penn Station's designers created a train station that could process more than 200,000 people a day. In 1945, 65 percent of intercity travel passed through the station; this dropped to 27 percent by 1960.

Considered an architectural masterpiece, the station opened in 1910. Since the train tracks were underground, the style of the station and passenger waiting areas could be considered more stylistic than functional. Passengers encountered the past and the future when they entered the station. Ancient Rome and all its glory encompassed the passenger waiting areas. Glass and steel structures throughout the concourse provided a glimpse of the future.

With the decline in passenger traffic, the Pennsylvania Railroad could no longer maintain that massive structure. The railroad would continue to operate its underground stations, but plans were developed to demolish the building. In its place would rise Madison Square Garden and Pennsylvania Plaza.

Preservationists, architects, and historians unsuccessfully fought to stop the demolition, which began in 1963. This loss of an iconic New York landmark led the Landmark Preservation Commission to establish protections for what residents deemed valuable. The eleven-member commission works with historians, archaeologists, researchers, preservationists, and lawyers to protect buildings and sites that are considered to be culturally, historically, and/or architecturally important to the city.

Another outcome of the destruction of Penn Station was opposition to a proposed Lower or Mid-Manhattan Expressway. Robert Moses planned a highway that would have been built through the center of the city. In its way were SoHo and Greenwich Village. The negative reaction to the plan caused it to fail.

New York experienced other setbacks during the 1960s. The economic growth that occurred after World War II peaked. Technological advances caused many of the city's factories to become outdated and too costly to operate. A shift in where goods were produced caused factories to move or close. New York Harbor experienced a decline in business. Its harbor was too small to handle container shipping; that business moved to New Jersey. The Brooklyn

Navy Yard was decommissioned by the US Navy in 1966, adding to the city's deteriorating economy.

Unrest over social issues and the war in Vietnam led to riots, protests, and strikes. The New York race riots of 1964 occurred in Harlem. Fifteen-year-old James Powell was shot and killed by a White off-duty police officer. Two days of peace protests followed the shooting.

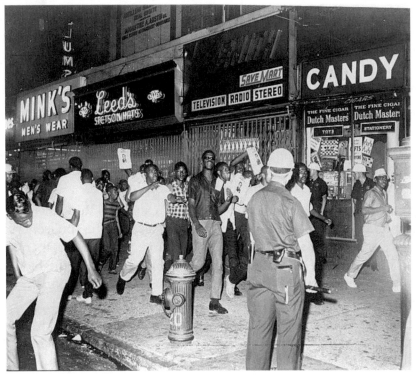

Demonstrators during the New York race riots.
https://commons.wikimedia.org/wiki/File:Demonstrators-Harlem-1964.jpg

On the third day, residents demanded the officer's termination or resignation. Tensions between the protesters and police mounted and became violent. Police officers tried to subdue the growing crowd with their nightsticks; protesters began to throw rocks and bottles at the police. The riots continued for five days. Stores were looted, fires were set, and windows were broken. There was one death, and hundreds were arrested.

Protests over the United States' involvement in Vietnam were led by Martin Luther King Jr. On April 15th, 1967, King and 400,000 others demanded an end to the country's role in Vietnam. Protesting from

Central Park to the United Nations, the activists demonstrated against the war. At that point, it was the largest protest against the war.

Demanding better wages and benefits and the lack of a contract caused more than seven thousand sanitation workers to strike in 1968. For nine long days, garbage accumulated along the city's streets until the workers' demands were met.

More turbulence continued in the city; teachers walked off the job, police officers called for a slowdown in arrests, and firefighters threatened to take action.

In June 1969, riots erupted at the Stonewall Inn located in Greenwich Village. In New York City, homosexual acts were illegal in 1969. Bars that served and welcomed gays, lesbians, and transgender people were often raided by the police, such as the Stonewall Inn.

Early in the morning, police raided the Greenwich Village bar with a warrant to search for illegal alcohol and violations of the state's gender-appropriate clothing law. Thirteen people were arrested.

People had had enough of the mistreatment. Residents of the neighborhood and other patrons fought against the police. When violence broke out, some police officers, those who had been arrested, and a writer from *The Village Voice* locked themselves in the Stonewall Inn. Some in the crowd tried to light the bar on fire. Eventually, those inside the bar were freed, and the crowd disbanded.

However, on and off for the next five days, riots and protests occurred at Stonewall Inn on Christopher Street and in Christopher Park, which was located nearby.

One year later, protesters marched from Stonewall Inn to Central Park in support of gay rights. The Christopher Street Liberation Day parade is considered the first gay pride parade in the country.

Chapter 10 – Standing Strong

The country's economic growth stalled and sputtered throughout the 1970s. During the decade, people experienced high rates of inflation and inconsistent economic growth, which was termed stagflation. An oil embargo tripled the price of crude oil by the end of the decade. It may go without saying, but uncertain times plagued New York City during the 1970s.

Manufacturing losses that started in the 1960s persisted as companies vacated the city. Estimates of up to one thousand businesses left the city from 1969 through the middle of the decade, which resulted in the loss of up to half a million jobs. Residents fled to the suburbs; up to one million people moved from New York to seek employment and safer neighborhoods. Over eleven thousand housing units were lost in the city to demolition or neglect.

Crime increased. Many began to view New York City as an unsafe place to live or visit. The murder rate in the city doubled from the mid-1960s to the mid-1970s, as did assaults and car thefts. Rapes increased threefold, and robberies increased ten times. A group calling themselves the Council for Public Safety published pamphlets warning residents of the dangers in the city and cautioning visitors to avoid the city.

Emblematic of the city's struggles in the 1970s was the multitude of fires that destroyed many neighborhoods in the Bronx. A number of factors contributed to the fires. One was the practice of redlining, which is now illegal. Red lines were drawn on maps to denote less affluent and racially mixed or non-White neighborhoods. These were viewed as risky investments, which disqualified them for insurance and loans.

Neighborhoods in the South Bronx, Bedford-Stuyvesant, Harlem, the Lower East Side, Brownsville, and Bushwick were among those often redlined. This meant that landlords and residents did not qualify for home loans or insurance to protect the buildings. These aging structures were frequently already in need of repair.

Additionally, the city was in a dire financial situation. One way that New York City leaders sought to save money was to lay off city workers. Closing "unneeded" fire stations would reduce government spending. The city hired the Rand Corporation to analyze the efficiency and response times of fire stations. With that data, the city could shutter fire stations that were redundant and no longer necessary.

However, the compilation and analysis of the data was faulty. Twelve fire companies were closed in the South Bronx, which led to long response times to small fires that quickly burned out of control. Estimates of forty fires a day burned throughout the area. Some neighborhoods lost 97 percent of their housing due to fire and neglect. Overall, during the 1970s and early 1980s, more than 250,000 people lost their homes and were forced to move.

New York City's fiscal crisis caused its leaders to borrow substantial amounts of money. Loans were needed to replace lost revenues from residents and businesses fleeing the city. Even with budget cuts, such as the closure of neighborhood fire stations, the gap between the city's operating budget and its income continued to widen. By 1975, the city was facing bankruptcy. Banks refused to lend the city any more money until it started repaying its debts.

New York City had a loan repayment of over $450 million due in October 1975. At that point, the city only had $34 million available. Concessions from the unions, hiring freezes, a guaranteed bond, and increasing charges for tuition, subways, and other services from the federal government were needed to avert a complete shutdown of the city.

One major construction project opened its doors while New York City battled fiscal uncertainty. The World Trade Center was controversial before and after its construction. Ideas about creating an international trade facility had swirled since the 1939 World's Fair, where there was an exhibit that illustrated the concept of peace throughout the world through worldwide trading.

However, the concept was not deemed viable until David Rockefeller pursued it. He created the Downtown Lower Manhattan Association, or DLMA, in 1958. Rockefeller sought a new location for the headquarters of Chase Manhattan Bank. As vice president of Chase's planning and development, Rockefeller wanted to retain and increase white-collar jobs in the Wall Street area. Additionally, Chase Bank already had a presence, and his family had real estate investments in the financial district of the city.

A firm was hired to analyze the feasibility of the project. However, McKinsey & Co. did not support the practicality of the creation of a world trade area. Rockefeller ignored the advice. Since he led DLMA, the idea proceeded. Rockefeller consulted with Robert Moses about the concept. Moses suggested that the redevelopment plan needed to be broad enough in scope to bring more construction projects to Lower Manhattan.

With Moses's backing, Rockefeller was able to obtain approval to take the needed land. In return, Chase Bank would support Moses and his ideas for the Lower Manhattan Expressway.

Rockefeller then began securing the support of Austin Tobin, who headed the Port Authority, to pursue the World Trade Center project. With the backing of the Port Authority, Rockefeller would have more avenues to secure financing for the project. Additionally, a public authority could seize property needed for construction under Title I of the Housing Act and eminent domain. Also, the application of building codes differed for public authorities and private construction.

Next, Rockefeller and the DLMA had to obtain support from the governors of New York and New Jersey. New York's governor at the time happened to be David's brother, Nelson, who backed the project. Later, critics of the World Trade Center mockingly referred to the towers as David and Nelson. New Jersey's governor, Richard Hughes, only agreed after the Port Authority assumed control of the struggling Hudson & Manhattan Railroad. New Jersey's governor also secured a transit hub location for the state's commuter rail line.

In 1962, Tobin formed the World Trade Department as part of the Port Authority. The first step before construction could commence was to obtain the land and then clear it. To accomplish that feat, streets and neighborhoods had to be "de-mapped." De-mapping removes existing streets from maps as though they never existed.

One targeted area that was needed for the towers housed Radio Row, a flourishing commercial neighborhood with many electronics stores. Residents and businesses sought to block the project by requesting an injunction from a state judge. To garner public support, protesters marched through the streets with a coffin that denoted the death of small businesses.

The lawsuit was thrown out by the US Supreme Court in 1963. Despite the objections, sixteen acres of land were seized by the Port Authority through eminent domain.

Residents were concerned with overbuilding since there were numerous office spaces available. Also, with the city's unhealthy economy, unneeded real estate would devalue current real estate.

The Committee for a Reasonable World Trade Center was formed in 1968 by Lawerence Wren. His group advocated for towers that were limited to nine hundred feet. To make their point, an ad was placed in *The New York Times*. In the ad, the president of the Allied Pilots Association alerted the public to what they viewed as safety issues. Congestion in the skies and the proposed height of the towers would necessitate alterations in flight patterns.

To illustrate their concerns, an artist drew a vivid image of a commercial airplane that was just about to crash into the upper levels of the North Tower. The North and South Towers both reached well beyond the committee's hoped-for nine hundred feet. Commercial airplanes would purposefully fly into both towers years after they opened.

None of the critics were able to thwart the building of the World Trade Center. Construction began on August 5th, 1966. Due to the height of the towers, work for the first two years was below street level; the foundations went seventy feet down to bedrock. The towers began their skyward ascent in 1968.

Excavation of WTC site.

More than 1.2 million cubic yards were removed from the site. This excavated earth added over twenty-three acres of land to the city. Vast quantities of construction materials were consumed in the formation of the tubular-shaped buildings. More than 200,000 tons of steel, 425,000 cubic yards of concrete, 2.2 million square feet of aluminum sheeting, and 600,000 square feet of glass were used in the creation of the Twin Towers.

The North Tower, or One World Trade Center, was partially completed in 1970 and opened for tenants on its lower floors. By 1972, the upper levels were finished. The South Tower, or Two World Trade Center, was completed in 1973. At the time of their opening, the towers were the tallest buildings in the world, with 110 floors each.

From the South Tower's observation deck on a clear day, visitors could see for forty-five miles. From its opening until its destruction, the observation deck welcomed almost forty-seven million people to partake in the viewing experience.

Significant damage occurred to the underground garage of the Twin Towers when terrorists attacked on February 26th, 1993. Built with 1,200 pounds of urea nitrate, the terrorists had hoped to destroy the towers; however, neither tower was damaged. Six people were killed in the bombing, and more than one thousand others were injured.

Within one month, the towers were fully reopened to business and visitors. Less than eight years later, both towers would be destroyed.

Early morning flights from Boston's Logan Airport on September 11th, 2001, were hijacked by terrorists. After taking control of the cockpit, the terrorists were able to divert American Airlines Flight 11 and United Airlines Flight 175 and fly both planes to New York City. Both flights had been headed to Los Angeles, California, so these planes were laden with fuel, which maximized the impact of the attack on the towers.

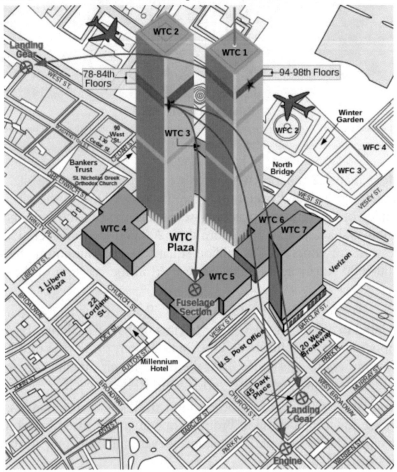

Diagram of WTC and 9/11 attacks.

Two other planes were also hijacked that morning. Terrorists flew a plane into the Pentagon; another crashed in a Pennsylvania field after some passengers tried to divert the plane.

Seventy-six passengers and eleven crew members were on board Flight 11 when five hijackers flew it into the North Tower. Everyone on the plane died upon impact. People working in the tower above the ninety-first floor were trapped in their offices.

News reports of a plane flying into the North Tower were quickly shown on live television. Many at the time assumed it was a small aircraft that lost control and accidentally flew into the building.

Millions of people saw the second plane hit the South Tower on live television. All fifty-one passengers and nine crew members died on impact when the plane flew into the building at 9:03 a.m.

Both towers were designed to withstand a plane flying into them. However, the heat from the fires caused structural damage. The upper floors collapsed into the lower floors. At 9:59 a.m., fifty-six minutes after being struck by Flight 175, the South Tower collapsed. By 10:30 a.m., the North Tower was gone. Falling debris from the Twin Towers contributed to the collapse of the five other buildings located at the World Trade Center.

Crowds of people ran from the burning buildings. Clouds of smoke filled the air. Debris fell from the falling buildings. People tried to outrun the danger. Thousands of people rushed to the city's aid. Firefighters, police officers, and healthcare workers ran toward the buildings to save those who were trapped inside and under the debris.

Within twenty-four hours, rescuers had recovered all the survivors. Almost three thousand people died in the collapse of the World Trade Center. Included in the causalities were over four hundred police officers and firefighters who entered the burning wreckage to assist those who were trapped. For weeks and months afterward, family members of the deceased searched for their loved ones.

Efforts to clear the site and recover the bodies were hampered by fires that burned for more than three months after the devasting attack. Unstable rubble created additional hazards for the crews. Site cleanup continued until May 2002. In total, over 1.8 million tons of wreckage was removed from Ground Zero. More than 108,000 truckloads of rubble were transported to a Staten Island landfill.

First responders, residents of the area, and cleanup crews were exposed to numerous toxins. Most did not have personal protective equipment to mitigate the effects of their contact with asbestos, fiberglass, freon, benzene from jet fuel, lead, and other toxic hazards. Respiratory illnesses, cancer, kidney issues, and heart diseases afflicted many of the people who assisted the city in its recovery.

In addition to painful and deadly illnesses, responders and thousands of others who witnessed the attacks suffered from and continue to live with post-traumatic stress.

Part of the recovery process for New Yorkers included looking to the future. To coordinate the honoring of the victims of the terrorist attacks and to rebuild, Mayor Rudy Giuliani and Governor George Pataki created the LMDC, or Lower Manhattan Development Corporation. They sought to create a memorial that would ensure the lives of those who died on February 16th, 1993, and September 11th, 2001, will be remembered and honored. The LMDC sponsored the World Trade Center Site Memorial Competition. Over 13,500 designs were submitted. Applications were received from each of the fifty states and ninety-four other countries.

Michael Arad's creation of *Reflecting Absence* was selected as the design that best captured the emotions for this memorial. In the space where each of the towers previously stood, two reflecting pools were created. Each pool is bordered by bronze panels on which are inscribed the names of the victims of the terrorist attacks. Names are arranged by where each person was on the day the towers fell.

Over four hundred trees were planted on the eight-acre site. The placement of trees designed by landscape architect Peter Walker includes the Survivor Tree. Seriously damaged during the 9/11 attacks, the Callery pear tree was relocated from the site. After being nurtured back to health, the Survivor Tree was replanted as part of the memorial. On the tenth anniversary of the attacks, the memorial site was opened to the public.

A second competition was held to determine the best path forward to rebuild the site. Daniel Libeskind's Memory's Foundations was selected. The feature component was his 1,776-foot-tall skyscraper to commemorate the signing of the Declaration of Independence and the rebirth of New York City. From Libeskind's original design to actual construction, many elements were altered to address safety and security concerns. Freedom Tower, now called One World Trade Center, opened in November 2014.

The tallest building in the Western Hemisphere, One World Trade Center's 104 floors stretch toward the sky. All four sides of the iconic landmark welcome visitors and those who work in its incredible office spaces. Towering sixty-foot-tall entrances create a flow from inside the building to the treelined plazas and reflective areas adjacent to the building.

A mere forty-seven seconds are needed to ascend the building in its SkyPod elevators and access the observatory. Opened in 2015, One World Observatory provides visitors with expansive vistas of the Brooklyn Bridge, which spans the East River. Other memorable and notable landmarks that can be seen from the highest location in the city are the Statue of Liberty, the Empire State Building, and the Flatiron Building. On clear days, all five boroughs are visible.

In addition to viewing upward and outward, visitors can gaze into the Sky Portal from the observation floor of One World Trade Center. Gazing through the fourteen-foot circle of glass, viewers can experience the sight of one hundred floors below them.

Post-industrial recycled materials were used and totaled 40 percent of all of the material needed to build the tower. Steel was fabricated from 95 percent recycled materials. The building was constructed with green concrete, which was created from waste from coal plants. More than 30 percent of all materials were from within five hundred miles of the construction site.

Bordering One World Trade Center are four other towers, the September 11 Memorial, and the September 11 Museum. Approaching the building, visitors will experience the sense of a partially collapsed building. The intent is to transition viewers from the falling towers to remembrances of those who died to the hopes of a brighter future. Visitors from all 50 states and over 175 countries have walked through the museum.

Once visitors enter the museum, they descend into the immense space that housed the Twin Towers and other buildings of the World Trade Center complex. At the base of the ramp is the Survivors' Staircase, which was used by those who were able to evacuate from the collapsing buildings.

Picture of the Survivors' Staircase.

Mark Kent, CC BY-SA 2.0 <https://creativecommons.org/licenses/by-sa/2.0>, via Wikimedia Commons; https://commons.wikimedia.org/wiki/File:Survivors_Staircase_2015_vc.jpg

Also displayed in the Foundation Hall is the Last Column. This was the final piece of steel preserved and retained from the wreckage of the World Trade Center. The column is covered with the signatures of and messages from Ground Zero cleanup workers. Once the column was removed from the site, a ceremony was conducted that signified the final step in the recovery.

A portion of a concrete retaining wall that was constructed to contain the waters of the Hudson River during the excavation of the site provides the frame for Foundation Hall. The slurry wall survived the terrorists' attacks and is included in the museum to represent the power of the city and its residents to survive and rebuild.

Historical exhibits ensure the lives of those lost on 9/11 and due to illnesses contracted from the rescue and cleanup will never be forgotten. These include pictures, artifacts, and audio and video recordings.

One World Trade Center.
Tobias Wrzal, CC BY 2.0 <https://creativecommons.org/licenses/by/2.0>, via Wikimedia Commons;https://commons.wikimedia.org/wiki/File:OneWorldTradeCenterOctober.jpg

Conclusion

Throughout its history, New York City has impacted people all over the world. For many people, the city is an inspiration and beacon of hope. For others, New York illustrates the disparities between rich and poor. Whatever your view of the city is, New York has influenced and continues to shape the country.

As home to Wall Street, New York impacts the financial markets of the nation and the world. As the headquarters of the United Nations, New York welcomes people from every corner of the globe and helps shape world policies and opinions. Broadway, the Metropolitan Opera, jazz clubs, and museums preserve culture.

The Statue of Liberty and Ellis Island symbolically welcome all. Neighborhoods and their residents prove the spirit of New Yorkers are resilient and will come together in difficult times.

Here's another book by Captivating History that you might like

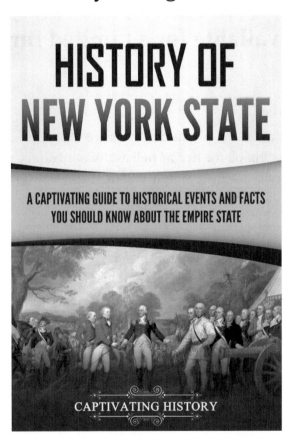

Free Bonus from Captivating History (Available for a Limited time)

Hi History Lovers!

Now you have a chance to join our exclusive history list so you can get your first history ebook for free as well as discounts and a potential to get more history books for free! Simply visit the link below to join.

Captivatinghistory.com/ebook

Also, make sure to follow us on Facebook, Twitter and Youtube by searching for Captivating History.

Sources

Ades, Lisa, Burns, Ric, and Sanders, James. *New York: An Illustrated History.* 2021.

Anbinder, Tyler. *City of Dreams: The 400-Year Epic History of Immigrant New York.* 2017.

Homberger, Eric. *The Historical Atlas of New York City, Third Edition.* 2016.

Koeppel, Gerard. *City on a Grid: How New York Became New York.* 2017.

New York Historical Society. https://www.nyhistory.org/.

Made in the USA
Thornton, CO
11/29/24 16:29:16

f56b1a59-7631-4226-b63f-5e3b014f38a8R01